EARLY
PROSE WRITINGS

Published @ 2017 Trieste Publishing Pty Ltd

ISBN 9780649566891

Early Prose Writings by James Russell Lowell

Edited by Trieste Publishing Pty Ltd.
 Cover @ 2017

www.triestepublishing.com

JAMES RUSSELL LOWELL

EARLY
PROSE WRITINGS

 Trieste

James Russell Lowell in 1843

Early Prose Writings
of
James Russell Lowell

With a Prefatory Note by Dr. Hale, of
Boston, and an Introduction by
Walter Littlefield

Published by John Lane
The Bodley Head
London & New York

Contents

Prefatory Note
By Dr. Hale
of Boston ❦

I HAVE hardly an earlier recollection of my college life than those which are associated with Lowell. I was very young in college, and for three years I lived with my brother who was in the class in advance of mine. He was very intimate with Lowell, who was his classmate,—three months younger than he. I think that in their sophomore year Lowell was still living in his father's house, at Elmwood,—a mile distant from the college. Afterward he had his room quite near us. But at the time of which I speak, when Lowell was a sophomore, he and my brother would come in together after recitations,—would very likely study together,—would be arranging for meetings of the I. O. H., which was a literary society,—or the Institute of 1770, or of the Puddings or the Harvard Union,—and when 1837 came would be getting up the numbers of the Harvardiana.

The fourth volume of the Harvardiana was edited by Lowell, Hale, Scates, King and Lippitt, all of the Harvard class of 1838.

I have said, in public, a hundred times, that
we knew as well, in 1838, when Lowell graduated, that he was to be a distinguished poet,
widely esteemed, highly valued in the literature
of the land, as we have since known that he
had won that position. As nobody has as yet
contradicted me, I will repeat that statement
here,—as well founded,—and not merely the
association of college friendship. Literature, I
think, was more cared for and perhaps more
highly valued in the college circles than it is
now. Certainly the public opinion of the little
" seminary " drifted in the lines which sug-
gested the study of the authors of one race and
of one time. Longfellow came to us before
Lowell was half through college. He was
cordiality itself in his intimacy with us boys,
—and if Lowell had needed any stimulus in the
study of the Continental masterpieces Longfellow's advent would have supplied it. But he
did not. And every appreciation and every
circumstance of his early life had led him to
the kind of reading which occupied his under-

graduate life. Mrs. Putnam, his older sister, who had much of the charge of his childhood, told me that when he was almost a baby,—when he still took a daily nap in his cradle,—she entertained the boy by reading " The Faerie Queene " to him to his great delight.

While we were in college there appeared to us some of the young gentlemen from New York who were most interested in establishing Alpha Delta Phi, as a literary society which should affiliate the better students of many American colleges. Among the editors of Harvardiana of that year were Wheeler, Haywood, Hildreth, who became charter members of this new society,—and at the proper time they added to their number the young men whom I have named,—who became their successors in the editing of Harvardiana. I was one of the next year's members,—and I suppose there is no harm in my saying that at the earlier meetings of Alpha Delta I heard Lowell read papers on the old English dramatists,—which are the basis of what he published afterwards in The Boston Miscellany.

Indeed in those undergraduate days he spent a great deal of time in the college library,—and was studying the masters of the early English dramas. " Beaumont and Fletcher," and " Massinger " are two of these papers. The fourth volume of Harvardiana is the last volume. The five editors wrote three-fourths of it. The other students criticised,—but did not often contribute. I doubt if three hundred copies were printed of any number.

Lowell's father's health and his mother's compelled their absence in Europe in 1837 and 1838. Mr. George Ellis used to tell this story of their winter in Rome,—when James Lowell was a senior.

" I was in Rome. I heard that Dr. Lowell had not received his American letters. I had received mine, so I went over to tell him the Boston news. I told him that my brother Rufus was to have the English oration at Commencement in James's class. I told him James had been suspended from college,—but I added that the class had chosen him their poet.

"'Oh dear!'—the old gentleman said. 'James promised me that he would quit writing poetry and go to work.'"

How many fathers would rejoice if their sons would make this promise! But how fortunate for another generation that "James" did not hold to his.

When they had graduated hardly twelve months, Bradbury and Soden, an ambitious pair of young men, proposed "The Boston Miscellany," a new magazine, of a literary grade quite above anything of its time. My brother Nathan, Lowell's near friend, was the editor for the first year. He undertook this charge, with the loyal help of Lowell and his near friend, Story. Before long the new magazine absorbed "The Arcturus," a similar venture made in New York by Mathews and Duyckinck, in the same year. In one year The Miscellany published articles by the two Everetts, Hawthorne, Willis, Parsons, Walt Whitman, Mrs. Stowe, Mrs. Kirkland, Lowell and Story,—by my mother, my sister and my brother. This list justifies me in saying that its grade was above anything before that attempted. I think there was no number without a poem or essay by Lowell.

The story, not very strong, but bright, of " My First Client " is one of these papers. I think it is " founded in fact," as Miss Edgeworth would say. It ought not be supposed that Lowell was unprepared for his career as a diplomatist. He had studied at the law school and with his father's friend and his, Charles S. Loring—one of the leaders at the bar. He was fond of his profession,—and his public life afterwards gave many evidences that his early study was the careful study of a young man interested in his work.

EDWARD E. HALE.

Matanuck, Aug. 16, 1902.

James Russell Lowell
In 1842 ♉ ♉ ♉ ♉

THE early writings of a man of genius are usually unimportant. In the enthusiasm of academic youth concrete knowledge greatly outweighs experience. Otherwise charming impromptus are lead-laden with sophomoric pedantry and egotism. Later, experience tones and qualifies expression; the imagination is quickened; the early-acquired knowledge is relegated to its proper sphere of influence. In Lowell, at twenty-three, there is nothing pedantic or sophomoric. His first verses may halt, his poetic imagery may be trivial, but his prose is always sure-footed although his steps be light. He wrote for the readers of *The Boston Miscellany* his original impressions of the things he read, saw, or imagined, and before reflection or study had a chance to evoke opinions and judgments. He wrote as a tourist might write of the panoramic scenes which meet the eye in a foreign country, before any attempt is made to study the institutions there and the principles governing them. To the end of his days Lowell remained an impressionist; but he was always

striving to find logical cause for his impressions, and tireless in his efforts to arrive at
judgments.   That is why, I think, his first
impressions are as interesting as his final
judgments are important.   Upon the middle
ground it would be neither fair nor profitable
to trespass.

Lowell entered Harvard in 1834, at the
age of fifteen, from an excellent preparatory
school kept by a Mr. Wells, in Cambridge.
He continued to reside under the paternal
roof at Elmwood. This scholastic advance,
therefore, meant much less to him than it
would to others.   Nevertheless, the attractions
of old Harvard Hall exerted their influence
upon him.   He passed much of his time in
tranquil book-walled alcoves.   Often the college bell failed to arouse him; through the
open window, in summer, would come the
shouts of his mates at play, but Lowell, deep
in the old poets—French and English, and
later his dearly-beloved Calderon—would rarely
heed these things except when awakened to
the consciousness that his monthly reports

from the Dean would give his reverend father
distress. Meanwhile, he contributed vagrant
verse to the college paper. When his gradua-
tion approached the writing of the class poem
fell naturally to him. It was natural, too,
that his careless regard of college authority
should finally be brought home to him. In
June, 1838, he was rusticated and sent to
Concord. There, while waiting for the poem
to take shape, we find him discussing German
philosophy with his tutor, hearing Emerson
praise Landor, and forming life-long friendships with Dodsley's " Old Plays," Cotton's
" Montaigne," and Hakluyt's " Voyages." For
the first time he began to realize, what years
afterwards he expressed in his address on
" Books and Libraries ": " A college train-
ing is an excellent thing; but, after all, the
better part of every man's education is that
which he gives himself."

On receiving his A. B. degree he was forced
to the alternative of the law and the ministry.
He chose the former. For the two succeeding
years he worked with spasmodic faithfulness at

the Harvard Law School.   Still, he did not entirely abandon his muse, for he became a con-
tributor to *The Southern Literary Messenger*, and,
on more than one occasion, was tempted to sur-
render all hope for legal fame.   Once, in 1839,
he even made up his mind to do so, when chance
took him into the United States District Court
where Webster was trying a case.   Fired by the
great man's eloquence he returned to Cambridge
with a burning desire to master Blackstone before bed time.   But Sidney's " Defense of
Poesie " and Puttenham's " Art of English
Poesie " intervened, and the rash resolution of
the morning subsided before the gentle ministra-
tions of the old English verse makers.

With a curiously resigned air as to the inevit-
ableness of duty he received his degree of
Bachelor of Laws and was admitted to the Suf-
folk Bar in 1840.   He took lodgings in Boston,
so as to be nearer the office of Charles Greeley
Loring, where he was supposed to continue his
legal reading.   One may easily imagine, however, that he spent more time browsing in the
Old Corner Book Store or in the Athanæum

Library than he did in the crowded and ill-smell-
ing court rooms of the town.

Besides his parent's wish, he was not without another motive to succeed at law. Among
his friends in the " Band," a semi-organized club
of young people, charmingly written-up in Dr.
Hale's "James Russell Lowell and His Friends,"
was a young lady of Watertown, Miss Maria
White, whom Lowell described on first acquaintance as " a pleasing young lady who knows more
poetry than any one I am acquainted with. I
mean, she is able to repeat more." The friendship, formed in 1839, soon developed into love,
and early in 1841 their engagement was announced. It is doubtful if the lady, who loved
poetry for its sentiment and music, could have
done otherwise than add new inspiration to her
lover's muse. At the same time, a keen sense
of his own growing responsibility probably decided him to give the law impartial trial. He
opened an office in Court Street, nearly opposite
the old Court House, and waited for clients.
While waiting he wrote. But it was not with
legal forensics that his pen was occupied. Never-

theless, we find the idea gradually shaping itself
in his mind that the literary labourer was worthy
of his hire.   In writing to his legal preceptor
and friend, Loring, he thus refers to the editor of
The Southern Literary Messenger: " I don't
think I shall write any more for him.   'T is a
bad habit to get into for a poor man, this writing for nothing.   Perhaps if I hang off he may
offer me somewhat."

His enthusiasm, therefore, is not surprising
when we find him writing to the same friend a
few months later :   " I have already been asked
to write for an annual to be published in Boston, and ' which is to be a fair specimen of the
arts in this country.'   It is to be edited (sub rosa)
by Longfellow, Felton, Hillard, and that set.
Hawthorne and Emerson are writing for it, and
Bryant and Halleck have promised to write.
The pay for poetry is five dollars a page, at any
rate, and more if the work succeeds according
to the publishers' expectations."

In this year—1841—we also find him anxious
to publish a collection of his poems, and he thus
writes to a friend :   " Now if you will find how

much it would cost to print 400 copies (if you
think I could sell so many; if not, 300) in decent style (150 pages—less if printed closely),
like Jones Very's book, for instance, I could
find out if I could get an indorser. I should
not charge less than a dollar per volume—should
you? I don't care so much for the style of
printing, as to get it printed in any way."

And so "A Year's Life" was printed, and
one may readily imagine what pleasure its appearance gave the gentle lady in Watertown,
whom Longfellow was later to describe "as
frail as a lily and as fair." But "A Year's Life"
was of substantial use to the poet. The editor
of *The Southern Literary Messenger* began to pay
him for his work; he also contributed, for pay.
to *The Boston Post* and to *Graham's Magazine,*
That year he earned between three and four
hundred dollars by his pen. As 1841 drew to a
close, a coming event was discussed in literary
and book-selling circles in Boston, which, if it had
not the distinction first to inspire Lowell with
the idea of becoming a professional man of letters, at any rate, it made it possible for him to

do so. This was the publication of *The Boston Miscellany of Literature and Fashion*, owned and edited by Lowell's friend, Nathan Hale, Jr.

The Miscellany was a decided innovation in American periodical literature. It was a monthly magazine, the typographical form of which was a frank adaptation of the Moxon literary brochures, double column, with designed bordered pages, to the number of forty-eight. Among the writers whom Mr. Hale secured as regular or occasional contributors were Hawthorne, whose "Virtuoso's Collection" appeared in an early number; Edgar A. Poe, N. P. Willis; Walt Whitman; Elizabeth Barrett, whose "Cry of the Human" appeared in the November number; Edward and Alexander H. Everett; W. W. Story, later to win fame as one of the greatest sculptors of his day; W. A. Jones; Mrs. J. Webb, Mrs. Kirkland, Mary E. Hewitt; Thomas W. Parsons, famous in Florence if not in Boston as a keen interpreter of Dante; James T. Fields, and James Russell Lowell. The Hales— Sarah P., Nathan, Jr., and Edward—were also contributors, and the larger share of the book reviewing fell to their hands. Besides original matter there were translations, both in prose and verse, from the French, Spanish, German, and Italian.

To the first number (January 1842), James Russell Lowell contributed his sonnet on Keats, "To Perdita, Singing," and anonymously, "Agatha"; to the second, we find him presenting a sonnet and an ode; to the third he contributed two prose sketches "Getting Up" and "A Disquisition on Foreheads"; the fourth had as its *pièce de résistance* his first article on "The Old English Dramatists"; and in the fifth number is "The First Client," which is probably the first as well as the last piece of pure fiction which he ever published. During *The Miscellany's* existence of twelve months Lowell contributed to its pages about a dozen prose pieces, not including book reviews, and about the same number of poems. He also continued to write for *Graham's*, contributing many book reviews and a few poems.

Through a retrospect of sixty years the list of contributors to *The Miscellany* seems formid-

able enough ; but it must be remembered that
many of them, like Lowell, had yet their spurs
to win, while, with the exception of Edward
Everett, there was no name of the then commanding force of Longfellow, or Emerson among
them.   But if Mr. Hale failed to secure for his
pages, as he had hoped, the most eminent writers
of the time, he at least showed an extraordinary
amount of discernment in hitting upon those
who, later on, were to become conspicuous if
not great.

The Miscellany must have meant much to
Lowell, but less in an artistic, than in a pecuniary
sense.   It was by no means his ideal of what
a magazine of literature should be.   Still, it gave
him remunerative employment, and, knowing
personally nearly all his fellow contributors, it
must have been for him, as well as for others, a
sort of academy, where personal views, qual-
ified or emphasized by an intimate exchange of
ideas, could be set before the public in such a
manner that local taste in letters might be puri-
fied and elevated.   Both Lowell and Story would
have been elated to have the engravings, fashion

articles, and "light" literature eliminated, and they and others so far prevailed upon Mr. Hale that translations from the German and French and original sketches were brought forward as a protest against the undoubtedly trashy and senseless fiction which was appearing in contemporary periodicals. Several contributors, especially Edward Everett Hale and W. W. Story, tried their hand at brief imaginative and extravagant pieces. Their work, however, was not distinctive. Far better than either Lowell or Story, Nathan Hale, Jr., knew what was needed to make the magazine a success. He recognized the educational value of critical literature and high class verse, but he also realized that his readers could not subsist on these things alone— hence the engravings, hence the fashion articles, and hence the futile attemps at refined light literature. What *The Miscellany* really needed was a serial novel, a sustained romance of incident, rich with human interest. I imagine that Mr. Hale was restrained from securing one through the erudite shrugs of the shoulders of his young advisers, who would be prone to con-

demn everything that did not seem to smack of
letters.   His own ideas on the subject are not
to be mistaken.   As expressed to the readers of
The Miscellany in the first number they are de-
lightfully modern in sentiment :

" It needs no wild belief in the glories or the
truth of the ideal at the expense of the real, to
bid us cultivate and enjoy this acquaintance with
artificial lives.   It is among such shadowy beings that we find some of our warmest friends.
We speak of their trials, their loves, their triumphs, as facts, as they are, despite their veil of
circumstance. Ophelia, Desdemona, the broken-
hearted Bride of Lammermoor, are they not real,
and our friends ?   Could we better nourish our
feelings of reverence for, and delight in, the
beautiful, the gifted, and the true, than we do
by the converse and the confidence of those true
men and women, who move in that artificial life
we find in books ?   The mind, and if not that,
the heart tells us easily what of all these *are*
'true ; and their society we may enjoy, in their
sympathy and love we may revel, though friends
who are thought to have a more real existence

may have grown cold or cruel, and castles, which had a more earthly foundation, have toppled to the ground."

It may seem strange that under such auspices and with such encouragement Lowell did not make a serious attempt to write fiction. "The First Client" shows that he did try his hand at it, in a modest way. This isolated instance plainly indicates that the fact was father to the thought. Dr. Hale is very likely right in his playful observation regarding it : " I guess at the bottom it was true. I think that when the painter who had painted his sign came in with his bill, Lowell thought for a moment that he had a client. Out of this he spun an amusing short story."

Parenthetically, it seems worth while noting here what Longfellow wrote in his diary under date of Nov. 29, 1852 : " Met Lowell in the street and brought him home to smoke a pipe. He had been to the bookseller's to buy a blank book to begin a novel, on the writing of which his mind is bent. . . . Lowell will write a capital novel." A fortnight later Longfellow

recorded that " Lowell came in.   He has begun
his novel."   In 1864, Lowell wrote to James T.
Fields, who had succeeded him as editor of *The
Atlantic Monthly*, and who now begged a novel
from his pen :   " I can't write one nor conceive
how any one else can."   It is apparent, however, that he reconsidered his abrupt declination
for he actually did begin " a sort of New England autobiography which " he thought " may
turn out well."

And so, perhaps after all, the influence of Mr.
Hale's ideas of fiction were not entirely lost to
Lowell even though he was never able to test
their value in a personal, practical way.   The
salient causes of his despair of fiction were just
as dominating in 1842 as they were later.
Lowell loved nature, and was always susceptible
of the charms of her outward manifestations,
paradoxical or otherwise, but man, as a psycho-
logical study, never strongly interested him.   He
never turned his back upon society, but he never
freely or willingly sought it.   He accepted
friendships, and sincerely did his part toward
maintaining them, but, as far as I have been able

to discover, he never attempted to gauge mental
attitudes, or to search for the cause of human
idiosyncrasy beyond what was clearly obvious
through word or action.   From those hours of
surreptitious seclusion in the alcoves of old
Harvard Hall, until the end of his days, he was
essentially a bookman.   "Scriptor sum ; scrip-
tum nihil alienum a me puto," he might truly
have declared of himself, with a slight yet sig-
nificant paraphrase of Terence.   The people in
great books he knew well: their creators he
knew better; neither evoked in his mind any
other desire than to be their faithful interpreter.
Again, even if he had been an observer of life,
his artistic, rather than scholarly habits, were
entirely averse to the constant labour of logical,
coherent thought, necessary for a long, sustained
flight of purely imaginative prose.   Had he written verse with less facility, it is likely that his
longest poems would never have been penned.

With the December number of *The Miscellany*,
Mr. Hale withdrew from the directorship of the
periodical in order to help his father edit *The
Boston Daily Advertiser*, and its destinies were

immediately merged into those of *The Arcturus of New York.* It was then that Lowell and his friend Robert Carter founded *The Pioneer,* which, as a magazine of literature and art, with no appeal to popular taste or stimulus for public fancy, succumbed at the end of its third number, with all the dignity that had attended its birth and characterized its brief life. It was merely a continuation of *The Miscellany* with the latter's possible saving features piously eliminated.

Mr. Hale, as I have said, fully appreciated the value of the novel both for itself and as a means of attracting readers to instructive literature, even though he was not permitted fully to expound his theory. Mr. Lowell, in his prospectus, not only declined to make any concession to the popular taste, then prevailing, but attempted to dictate to the great reading public. He promised that *The Pioneer* should " furnish the intelligent portion of the reading public with a rational substitute for the enormous quantity of thrice-diluted trash, in the shape of namby-pamby love tales and sketches, which are monthly poured out to them by many of our popular magazines."

This is as striking a revelation of the man's literary ideas as it is of his ignorance of human nature. N. P. Willis showed marvellous perception when he wrote:

" J. R. Lowell, a man of original and decided genius, has started a monthly magazine in Boston. The first number lies before us, and it justifies our expectations,—namely, that a man of genius who is merely a man of genius, is a very unfit editor for a periodical."

*   *   *   *

With the exception of the final essays in each part of this volume the material herein contained appeared in *The Boston Miscellany*. The article on the plays of Thomas Middleton and that on Song Writers, were first published in *The Pioneer* in 1843. The articles on the Elizabethan dramatists—Chapman, Webster, Ford, and Massinger—were, in 1845, thrown into the form of conversations, and, together with a long dialogue on Chaucer, published in a volume called "Conversations on the Old Poets." This volume was reprinted in a revised edition in 1846. It also made its appearance in a London reprint in 1845 or '46. All editions of it are now very rare. In 1887, Lowell delivered a series of Lowell Institute Lectures in Boston on " The Old English Dramatists." These were published in book-form, after the author's death, in 1892.

On three distinct occasions, therefore, Lowell publicly expressed himself concerning the Elizabethans. In his riper years he utterly ignored *The Boston Miscellany* articles, and adversely criticised the " Conversations," partly through a sense of their literary shortcomings, and partly because he wished his later judgments to stand. This was only natural. His literary executor Charles Eliot Norton, his semi-official biographer Horace E. Scudder, and his authorized publishers Messrs. Houghton, Mifflin, & Co., have religiously respected his wishes on this point. Lowell's initial ideas concerning the Elizabethans have been called of youth, youthful. It has been pointed out that the opinions in the " Conversations " have, in many cases, been utterly reversed in the Lowell Lectures ; that

the non-critical articles in *The Miscellany* were
entirely unworthy to be associated, even remotely,
with what Lowell later did in imaginative or
didactic prose.

If this be true, what excuse is there for drag-
ging his frailties from their dread abode at this
hour? Why should the public be invited to ex-
amine what Lowell himself was indifferent to
and what his literary sponsors have condemned?
Or, if it has been deemed right to rake up any
remote literary remains, why has the humble
grave of *The Miscellany* been selected by the
prowling ghoul rather than the more sump-
tuous sepulchre of the "Conversations"?

But is it not possible that the point of view of
both his literary executor and his biographer may
be slightly distorted through a too ardent desire
to carry out the supposed wishes of the dead and
to conserve his fame in the best possible light?
Lowell's indifference to his early prose writings
is readily explicable by the fact that he was
conscious of having extended himself beyond
their narrow confines, and this feeling, trans-
mitted to his friends, assumed the proportions of

deep-rooted conviction against which there is no appeal. Again, although the " Conversations " contain opinions and judgments which Lowell was later to modify, replace, or reverse, the articles on the Elizabethan dramatists, in *The Miscellany*, do not. They are simply the impressions of a youth of strong literary tastes who, discovering for himself a new field for inspiration and intellectual delight, would make his readers partakers of his joys of possession. As for the other material drawn from *The Miscellany* and included in this volume, while being no mean work for a young man in his early twenties, it is of special interest as helping to reveal the ability upon which, at that time, Lowell based his intentions to forsake the bar and become a man of letters. It is imaginative, sensitive, and of considerable literary charm. Together with the essays on the Elizabethans it shows, as nothing else can, the formative influences that saved Lowell from becoming a "gentleman of the green bag." Neither the fame of the writer nor the literature which he loved so well and was later so richly to endow, will receive a blemish by the reproduction of these early efforts.   But, being the stone which the builders of his temple of fame have zealously rejected, they can never " become the head stone of the corner." I would simply rescue them from the shunned rubbish heap outside the official edifice and place them within a suitable enclosure where they may be examined with a proper appreciation of what they once meant to their author.

One word more.   In point of chronology and in the pleasantest, in the truest sense of the term, Lowell was the first complete American man of letters.   Longfellow had his professorship, Emerson his church, Hawthorne his clerk- ship, Irving his counting-house.   But Lowell, a briefless barrister, gave himself entirely to the profession of letters, seeking and gaining there the wherewithall for respectable maintenance, and in the very year that Washington Irving, on his highest wave of popularity, accepted the Madrid mission in order to eke out the richest pecuniary rewards that an American author had so far en- joyed.   Before the last number of *The Miscel- lany* left the press Lowell gave up his office in

Court Street. His apprenticeship to letters was complete. He was willing to abide by the destiny of his pen. Vacillation in purpose and task had given way to confidence and enthusiastic work. The best judges in the country had praised his verse and had discussed his prose. He still lacked, however, a mission. This he found in the temperance agitation of the late forties; in the Mexican War; in the Abolition movement; in the War of the Rebellion; and, later still, in national and international politics. Yet it is probable that he never seriously doubted that literature was sufficient unto itself and for himself.

WALTER LITTLEFIELD

New York, July 14, 1902

STORIES . SKETCHES . ESSAYS

The First Client:

With Incidental Good Precepts for Incipient Attorneys ♆ ♆ ♆

I SAT in my new attorney's office. I had just
been admitted to the venerable fraternity
of the Blank Bar. As I turned my admiring gaze from one part to another, I
thought—perhaps it was prejudice—that I
never saw a room into which, as from a natural
taste and instinct, the wronged and oppressed
portion of the community would flock more
readily. It seemed exactly suited to the circumstances and wants of that numerous and highly
respectable class of our fellow-citizens. It was
large, well-lighted, and of easy access. It had
no carpet, or any other sign of comfort or taste,
both of which are generally esteemed incom-
patible with extensive legal attainments. One
side was occupied by a large book-case, the green
silk behind whose glass doors made an impene-
trable mystery of the learning within, and whose
mahogany had assumed a sympathetic similitude
of hue with law-sheep.

And here let me indulge in a few words of
advice to the young counsellor who is hovering
in eager uncertainty between " that large and
commodious office, recently occupied by Increase

S. Sawder, Esq.," and "that pleasant apartment,
equally suitable for the artist or man of business,
and whose situation, within a stone's throw of
the post-office on the one hand, and the court-
house on the other, renders it so peculiarly
eligible." You are in a fluttering hurry of doubt.
You know that your fellow-student, Joe Bangs,
is on the lookout. The hope of catching some
stray clients of the great Mr. Sawder who belong to that excellent class, who, having once
found their way, by accident or design, into an
attorney's office, frequent the same forever there-
after, patronizing rather the locality than its
happy possessor, and fully satisfied of the excellence of the law administered there,—provided
the bust with the very dirty nose (the cabalistic
term " CICERO " imprinted thereon being, they
are firmly convinced, some classical allusion to
the merits of General Washington as a patriot
and soldier) still maintains its dignified stand on
the bookshelves,—the hope, I say, of securing
the patronage of some of these almost decides
you. At the same time you cannot but acknowledge the eligible situation of the other

office, " whose windows look upon a yard
tastefully decorated with lilac and other flower-
ing shrubs, thus combining the peculiar advantages of town and country life,"—and others,
for which " see advertisement." You feel a
secret, but unwillingly acknowledged, conviction,
that, if the vicinity to the eating-houses had been
properly set forth in the advertisement, you
would have been overcome. As it is, you con-
sult your friends. Factions arise, allusions to
meeting at Philippi are considered in order, and
you are farther from your decision than ever.

Now listen to an expert, as we say. Always
take the advice of the book-case. You stare,
but I am perfectly serious. If Jacques could
" find books in running brooks," I will lay ten
to one that he would be puzzled to find them
on the shelves of half the young lawyers in
practice, or in their heads either. Now one of
the two is necessary, the shelves perhaps the
more so. There is everything in the air of a
book-case. Never choose an office where there
is a book-case with a foolish face. There is as
much difference in them as in their employers.

One which, to the inexperienced eye, may appear of unexceptional character, shall yet seem uneasy, and, as it were, blush when a client stares at it, thereby exposing its vacuity by a look of conscious guilt. Another, just as empty, shall stand boldly up, and look bursting with unnumbered and unnumberable volumes of Coke and Blackstone, and other ponderously learned works of which most practitioners have barely heard, but which your book-case, if discreet, shall make the unwary client believe you have at your fingers' ends. Mine is one of these. In one remote and lonely corner of it nestles my economical law library, while its erudite air seems to assert positively that the few scattered volumes on my desk were crowded out for want of room.

This is one of my hobbies, and I see it has taken the bit between its teeth. I am not free to assert that a book-case is *all*. I only give it the chief place, and my young friends may be assured that a green booby of a book-case will eventually blunder out the secret entrusted to its charge. Next to them, in my judgment, stand

fire-proof safes. Get an office with a safe in
it, if possible. If empty now, it has yet a
prophetic fulness. It has at any rate a paulo-
post future air of papers too valuable to be
lightly risked. There is dignity in them at the
least, and an iron door left ajar with discrimi-
nating and deliberate carelessness, and disclosing
a file of papers secured with red tape, may perhaps sow a good seed in the imagination of a
client, and fill his mind with vague ideas of
future elevations to red cushioned benches. In
the most useless point of view, safes are worth
having. The locks are constructed with such
nicety that it is often both exhilarating and instructive to turn the bolt back and forth, and to
hide the beautifully polished key, which secures
such an infinite deal of nothing, in some unfind-
able spot.

There is much mystery in whiskers, also,
those dressed by a line drawn from the lower
tip of the ear to the corner of the mouth being
esteemed by good judges the most suitable.
Neither would I be so bold as to deny the effi-
cacy of a quick-set-hedge cut of the hair. Some

consider an occasional oath, if inserted with
grace and modesty, very advisable. I shall not
insist on their necessity, though Longinus
advocates them in his treatise on the sublime.*
You should always bear in mind, also, that the
only *opinions* a lawyer is supposed to have anything to do with are those he is paid for, or, which
is to the full as likely, charges for on his books,
—the term " books " being understood as meaning the blank pages in Dickinson's Almanac.
If he show symptoms of any others, clients are
first astonished, and then indignant, and friends
" are surprised that Thomas should have taken
up such notions," and consider their duty, as
good Christians and members of the church, to
starve the said Thomas into a better frame of
mind by bestowing their business on somebody
else who *has no mind* to injure his prospects in
this way.

If a client come in, it is always advisable to
be too busy to attend to him at first. Men are
ever most ready to put their affairs into the
hands of those who have too much to do to at-

*Section XIV.

tend to them faithfully. Always be finishing a letter to some imaginary lawyer in extensive practice in a distant city with regard to some possible John Smith, who has absconded, after defrauding an unfortunate washerwoman " out of four-and-sixpence, and a large family of children, all of them of tender age and excellent habits, having recently joined the association of reformed inebriates." This, I need not say to you, though you might to your client, is gratis business, and of course to be attended to before any other. Whenever you leave your office, let a placard on the door force upon the minds of all passers-by the hugely-written information that you are " IN THE S. J. COURT," or the " C. C. P.," or in any other place in the realm of fictitious narrative which is large and important enough to receive your learned person.

Having imparted all this valuable information, partly from pure benevolence, partly to show my experience, and partly my wit, I return to myself. I had been in my office a month. I had fourteen blank writs and other blanks in abundance, and my own face, from constant association, began to grow blank also. The writs were well enough in themselves, and the clerk's signature did him a great deal of credit ; but the morals of society had improved to such an alarming pitch that they remained blank, and seemed to forebode a tedious pertinacity in blankness and virgin purity. A friend, disguised as a substantial farmer without any bump of locality, had three several times enquired " if this were Mr. Mortmain's office " at every door on both sides of the street. Three times also, with a thick file of papers in my hand, I had hurried the same individual to and from the Court-House, in the most sidewalk-crowded parts of the day. Moreover I had generously made the same individual a free gift of the sum of ten dollars in one dollar bills, which he was obliging enough to return to me from a very greasy, apoplectic-looking calf-skin pocket-book, in Court street, counting with the usual delibera-tion of a thrifty agriculturist, and, between whiles, eulogizing my skill as a practitioner.

Still my door had not once opened unexpectedly.

I knew by sight every crack in my ceiling, and the peculiar expression of every paving-stone under the window. I imagined the pictures my " predecessor in office " had hung on the brass-headed nails he had left in the walls. I felt a curiosity about the foreigner with a moustache, who had twice passed up the street exactly at eleven, A. M. I could sit with my back to the window, and recognize every boy who cried the " Times " by his voice. I felt sorry when the boy with half a hat had caught cold, or the boy in the superabundant boots had overtasked his lungs to the blasting of his prospects for the rest of the day. I felt as if I had a kind of ownership and constabledom over them. I surmised from the expressions of their countenances those who were playing truant, or whose mothers were ignorant of their exotericity. They had restless eyes, and sat with a prospective uneasiness. I had my pet spiders, one in each corner of the room, and laid imaginary bets with myself as to the number of vacancies each would make in a week in my band of bluebottles (consisting exclusively of wind-instruments), whom

I maintained in humble emulation of the Emperor Nicholas's French-horn band. I knew familiarly all the men with pea-jackets who leaned all day against the lamp-posts. I thought of the doctrines of Pythagoras with even more respect, and concluded that in their former state of existence they had been lamp-lighters. I speculated upon the age required to entitle a man to green baize jackets, having observed that the wearers of them were a peculiar race, who had apparently come into the world in green jackets to illustrate Wordsworth's doctrine of "not in utter nakedness." That these garments are an artificial and not a natural appendage, nothing will ever persuade me.

The eyes of a man who has nothing to do are keen. I saw everything. I could tell by the expression of Hodge's face, as he stared at a highly-coloured engraving of a French species of woman in the picture-framer's window, that doubts had for the time arisen in his mind as to the correctness of his ideal of female loveliness, his theory of which was based wholly on " our Sally Ann." I was sure, for nearly five minutes,

that the man in the white hat and the brass
chain unsuggestive of any watch, was looking
for my office, and guessed he gave two cents for
the orange. I could not imagine who ate all the
molasses candy which the Irish woman in men's
boots had for sale, but supposed that Providence
appointed young ravens of one kind or another
for that useful duty. I came to a pretty well-
grounded opinion that the new bonnets were not
tasteful or becoming when they exposed the
whole crown and part of the back of the head.
I thought the French must be a queer-looking
nation if they resembled the plates of Paris
fashions in the tailor's window opposite, and
wondered if the said tailor knew how badly the
left-hand lower corner pane of glass was cracked.
I did n't see how people could eat pea-nuts, but
supposed they were used to it. I thought how
pleasant it would be in Greenfield now, and
was just starting for " the Glen " with a raptur-
ous party, when I was roused from my reverie
by a shadow against my glass door !

It was a client-like shadow. It had a well-
to-do-in-the-world look, and a litigating one

withal. It was a shadow that would pay well. It was perhaps a shadow that had a claim on the Ocean Insurance Office. I was sure it was not Peter Schlemihl's shadow, because that was pinned up forever in Hawthorne's "Virtuoso's Collection." That it was a shadow of a real man, admitted not the shadow of a doubt. My cottage in the country, with the white lilac and the honeysuckle in front, and the seat just large enough for two under the elm-tree, drew ten years nearer in as many seconds. I debated in my own mind the figure for the carpet in the back parlour, and decided to leave it to my wife. I determined if I met Jones, to buy that bay mare he had spoken of so highly. I should take little Tommy to the Boston Museum to see the man swallow himself (as he had done under the patronage of the Emperor of Russia, and several other great princes), and whom I thought the greater wonder, inasmuch as most men are such impostures that they must find it easier to make their friends swallow them than to do it themselves. And little Mary *should* have the rocking-horse, that was certain.

The door opened, and a man, whose face I dimly remembered, came in. He was certainly somebody I had met somewhere. It was very flattering in him to remember me. I asked him to take a chair, at the same time putting an easy arm-chair in the place of the very hard one with forward-sloping, slippery bottom, which I reserved for bores. He did not sit down, but, taking off his hat, eradicated a small file of papers from the mass of red bandanna and other merchandize which filled it, and, selecting one, handed it to me. It was doubtless a succinct statement of his case. I was right. It read as follows, and was a model of its kind:

Thomas Mortmain, Esq., to John Brown, Dr.

To 2 tin signs, at $1.00 . . .	$2 00
" 1 do. do.	1 25
" 1 sign-board	1 25
" painting and lettering do. 4 ft. at $1.50	6 00
" lettering name on glass . . .	50
	$11 00

Rec'd payment,   E. V.

Married
Men:
By One Who
Knows Them

DURING the honey-moon, as during courtship, few men display their real character. An artificial restraint is placed upon them, and, with few exceptions, in that brief period of felicity, they imitate as closely as possible the beau ideal of a pattern husband. But alas! the honey-moon too often sets in clouds—the mask soon falls, and the shades of character come darkly forth. The Titian tints of the portrait deepen into the sombre hues of Rembrandt, and the married man shows his true colours. It is then the task of the philanthropic and observant author to depict, with the utmost fidelity, the principal characteristics of some of the Benedicts. Let us begin, for instance with

THE ATTENTIVE HUSBAND.

You recognize the Attentive Husband at the very first glance. When he walks with his lady he carries her parasol and reticule, watches her with fearful anxiety, and expresses his fears that she is fatiguing herself; suggests the ex-

---

This article is an adaptation of a portion of a little French work by Charles Paul De Kock, which proved to be an intranslatable for more than one reason.

pediency of resorting to a cab or hack, and informs her that if he is walking too fast for her, he possesses the ability to moderate his progressive speed ; all of which profound and pertinent remarks are either heard in silence, or produce a scarcely perceptive elevation of the lady's shoulders, suggestive of impatience or annoyance. When he takes her to a lecture or a concert, she is naturally desirous of hearing the speaker or the singers, but our careful husband, in the midst of an interesting passage or a charming song, discovers that she looks pale, and inquires with much interest if she feels unwell. A simple negative is unsatisfactory. He enumerates a number of disorders, and she must defend herself by denying them separately and singly. At a dinner-party, no matter how far removed from the lady, the attentive husband fixes his vigilant eye upon her with a gaze as fearfully fascinating as that of the cobra capella. His remarks on such an occasion are generally unsatisfactory to the lady, as those of the physician were to Sancho Panza during his melancholy reign at Barratraria.

" My love ! don't think of eating that ! Good heavens ! anchovies are rank poison to you. It 's as much as your life 's worth. Don't give her Madeira, for the love of heaven. I know her constitution, sir."

The lady commonly puts an end to the affair, by coaxing her lips into a very pout, and eating nothing at all—opposition having spoiled her appetite. Meanwhile the careful husband proves himself a very commendable trencher-man ; eats freely of the forbidden fruits, and is by no means neglectful of the prohibited Madeira. If this happy couple are going to a ball, the watchful care of the attentive husband commences with the toilet.

" My dear child, that gown is too low in the neck—you will catch your death assuredly. Besides it is too tight—I know it is."

" I assure you, my dear, it is the very reverse."

"Ah ! you women will never confess it—pinch yourselves to death for the sake of fashion —and die martyrs to the ambition of having a small waist." Here the gentleman commonly

repeats the names of a number of ladies who
have fallen victims to a prevalent folly, and sub-
stantiates his statements with a world of circumstantial evidence.   He ends by declaring that if
the lady wears " that dress," he shall be very
unhappy, in fact, perfectly miserable, for the
entire   evening ;   whereupon   she   substitutes
another gown, which is very ill-made and very
unbecoming, and thinks all the evening of the
discarded dress, which fitted to a charm.   In the
ballroom, instead of permitting his wife to enjoy
herself, and seeking to pass the evening pleas-
antly himself, the attentive husband never loses
sight of his wife a single moment—not from
motives of jealousy, for the attentive husband is
never jealous, being fully persuaded that his lady
cannot find in the entire world a being so devoted to her welfare and happiness as himself;
but in the ballroom, as in the street, and at home,
he manifests the most untiring, and indeed
touching solicitude.   Sentinel-like, he paces to
and fro in the apartment where his wife is, and
she has no sooner finished a single dance, than
he accosts her :—

" You are very warm, my dear."

" Not too warm."

" Yes, too warm decidedly. Do you dance another quadrille ? "

" Certainly, I am engaged."

" My dear, you shock me unspeakably. You should never have accepted.   You should have rested yourself."

After the next dance, the moment her partner has handed her to her seat, the figure of her husband appears like one of those phantoms that arise so startlingly by the agency of Phantasmagoria.

" How red you look ! " exclaims the attentive husband, with the mournful air of a watchful mother, who suspects from the pulse of a child, the existence of fever.

The poor woman tries to smile as she replies, " Is there anything strange in having a colour after dancing ? "

" No, not a little colour I admit, but upon my soul, I never saw you look so feverish before."

An idea suddenly flashes across the mind of the poor woman, so mortifying and appalling that it visibly deepens the carnation of her cheek. Something whispers that her complexion approximates to that of a lobster, after its immersion in boiling water. She appeals to her next neighbour and ascertains it to be "a weak invention of the enemy."

A young gentleman having been so fortunate as to capture a couple of ice-creams, which a waiter is bearing by with very tantalizing rapidity, offers one to the wife of our attentive husband. The latter detects his partner in the very act of raising a spoon surcharged with a portion of the contents of the whip-glass to her lips. In an instant he is at her side, and with an air of triumph removes the dangerous glass from her fair hand.

"What were you thinking of?" he asks, with a half-tender, half-reproachful air.

"I was going to eat the ice," replies the pouting fair.

"Not one particle, my love. Ice after dancing? Monstrous! You are too warm—the ice too cold. It would be the death of you."

"But these ladies have all been dancing—and they are eating ices."

" These ladies may do precisely what they please. If they choose to tempt Providence, it is no concern of mine. An ice! oh! no indeed. I know your constitution."

And with these very consolatory remarks, the gentleman parades before his wife, sipping the interdicted luxury, with tantalizing spoon, and smack most satisfactory. Nor does he hesitate to say :—" Excellent! upon my soul — most excellent !" ⸳

In a few moments the orchestra commence a prelude of one of Strauss's magnificent waltzes. The lady, who is passionately fond of waltzing, accepts the arm of a young gentleman who is reputed a good waltzer, and they spin around the saloon to the admiration of the spectators; but no sooner does our attentive husband perceive the agreeable occupation of the lady than he rushes towards her, at the imminent risk of being prostrated by the throng of happy dancers, and seizing her by the arms, exclaims : " What are you about ? What are you thinking of ? How fortunate I came in time to prevent the continuance of this absurdity ! "

" But, my dear, you know I am passionately fond of waltzing."

" Very likely—but it does not agree with you. You will be sick to-morrow. I have consulted many medical gentlemen upon the subject, and they all assure me that waltzing is positively ruinous to ladies of a nervous temperament; so really I cannot permit it."

" But, my dear sir," ventures the young gentleman, " just a few turns."

" Once or twice round the saloon," chimes in the lady, with a supplicating air.

But the husband is inexorable. He takes his wife by the arm, leads her to a seat and throws a cloak, a mantilla, a pelisse, whatever comes to hand, over her shoulders, and then folds his arms, à la Napoleon, and surveys her with a look of tranquil triumph.

The lady dares not murmur. It would be bad taste to quarrel in public, and so as the attentive husband is the best of characters, she is looked upon by all the married women as being supremely happy. The supper hour is at hand. She has learned from the lips of her fair hostess, that the ladies only will be seated at the table, and she anticipates a pleasant repast, free from the assiduous attentions of her husband. Alas! how futile are her hopes! About fifteen minutes before supper is announced, he cheerfully presents himself, bearing his wife's cloak, in which he carefully envelopes her beloved form, while with an affable smile, he thus addresses her: " My darling, the carriage is waiting for us at the door."

" What! are you going so soon ? "

" So soon, my child! It is quite late."

" But supper will be ready in a moment."

" Aha! the very reason for our going. You might be tempted to eat something—and suppers are always unhealthy, particularly for so delicate a constitution as yours. No supper for you to-night," he adds, with a cheerful chuckle. " Come, my dear, the carriage is waiting."

He draws her arm within his own—that most attentive gentleman. She could weep, like Eve upon the threshold of Paradise, as she casts a " longing, lingering look behind," upon the brilliant supper-room, now glittering and

glowing with chandeliers, and plumes, and flowers, and diamonds, and bright eyes, and happy
faces. It fades like a vision, and as she enters
the gloomy carriage, she silently records a vow
to live henceforth the life of a nun, and give up
dinner-parties, balls, and all festivities. Can a
woman be happy with an *Attentive Husband?*
Happily the species is quite rare.

We will proceed, ladies and gentlemen, to exhibit another specimen of married humanity,
whose title, in the language of his natural enemy, the housemaid, is

THE BETTY.

A man is born a Betty, as he is a genius,
mechanician, musician, poet, or financier. The
Betty may adore his wife and children, be an
honourable man of business, and acquit himself
of all those duties which society imposes, but
his home will be disagreeable.

Breakfast is served. The wife takes up the
morning paper, while she sips her coffee, and
our domestic gentleman amuses himself by making toast. For a few moments he is absorbed

in silent contemplation of the glowing embers, but in a short time he calls the attention of his wife, and says, " did you put a stick of wood on the fire last evening, after I went out ? "

"A stick of wood, my dear ? What did you say ?"

" I was not talking Hebrew, I believe. When I went out last evening, at nine o'clock, there were two sticks on the fire, a large and small one—enough to last till bed-time. I don't want to prevent your having as much fire as you please, but I want to keep an exact account; for this morning I found three brands. Now, how could there be three brands if you did not burn a third stick ? "

" Ah! my dear, how vexatious you are, sometimes. I may or may not have put on more wood. I am trying to read an article which interests me, and you must needs interrupt me about a paltry stick of wood ! "

The domestic gentleman is silent, and contents himself with whistling to himself in a low tone, a thing which he is in the habit of doing, when he is dissatisfied with a reply.

At breakfast the butter arrests his attention.

" How much did you pay for this butter ? " he asks.

" I don't know, I'm sure."

" Don't know! Good heavens! what do you mean ? "

" The servant purchased it."

" You learned the price from her, of course ? "

" Yes, yes—I remember, it was thirty-six cents, I believe."

" You *believe!* Here! Sally, Sally ! "

The servant makes her appearance and is arraigned before the domestic man.

" How much was this butter, Sally ? "

" Thirty-six cents, sir."

" Thirty-six cents a pound ? "

" Of course—it was n't thirty-six cents a firkin," replies the young lady, with a disdainful and rather daring curl of the lip; and as she leaves the room, she indulges herself with the housemaid's luxury of slamming the door behind her.

" Thirty-six cents a pound ! " repeats the domestic man. " Thirty-six cents ! It is truly frightful to think of! I ate some capital butter at Bilson's the other morning, and he only paid thirty-two cents. Bilson's butter was the better of the two."

When the housemaid commences the daily task of sweeping the room—a duty which would seem to carry its reward with it, to judge by the cheerful zeal with which it is commonly performed, the domestic husband is always before the servant's broom, peering into every corner, solicitous to detect cobwebs, and pushing his scrutiny into every hole and corner. Some time before the dinner-hour he is accustomed to make a solemn tour of the kitchen. He is an habitual lifter of pot-lids, an inquisitor of tin-kitchens and reflecting bakers. If the old fashion of roasting meat is still honoured in his family, he draws his stool to the chimney-corner, and bakes the crown of his head as he bends over the fire, and whips up the turn-spit into a full gallop. He hovers over an unknown dish, in doubt awhile, and then summons the cook.

" What have you here ? "

" Fricasséed chicken, sir."

" Have you put in mushrooms ? "

" Certainly, sir."

" It is very singular—I can't find any. Ah !
here I have one—yes, yes, it 's all right. Do
we have soup to-day ? "

" Don't you see the pot on the fire ? "

" Very true. But let me tell you, you spoil
your soups by putting too many vegetables in
them. Now how many carrots have you put
in ? "

" I 'm sure I don't remember. Must I count
them now ? "

" It will be as well. Stop, I 'll do it for you.
I should n't be surprised if there were half a
dozen."

And the gentleman commences a painful
search for the orange-coloured vegetables, in the
course of which he receives sundry splashes
from the unctuous and savoury soup, and finally,
in tasting a spoonful of the compound rather
prematurely, he scalds his mouth severely, without however receiving the least sympathy from
the cook, to whom such an occurrence seems
to give peculiar satisfaction. An accident of

this kind usually puts an end to his quest, and he leaves the kitchen with diminished dignity. The Betty is the peculiar aversion of the cook. Indeed your cook seldom remains long in the service of your domestic man—she soon demands her wages and quits his roof—but the lady of the house is debarred the enjoyment of the servant's privilege—for such the scandalous world asserts that she considers it.

Getting Up

IGNORANT or misguided men are accustomed to bewail the difficulty of what is generally called (not perhaps without some homœopathic tincture of bitterness) " getting up in the world." But it seems to us that this faculty, if it may be so termed, comes, like honest Dogberry's reading and writing, " by nature." Men are born with it; and are sometimes haunted and dogged by luck to that degree that they long for a dash of reverse as a relief from an inevitable and intolerable bore. But even to those who are fated to labour up in the world, this toil is but an ant-hill beside the mountain labour of getting up in the morning. To one nestled warmly in his blanket, what an impertinence do all the uses of this world seem. " Getting up early," saith the octogenarian, " is the surest method of long life," and he himself stands like an undeniable text of holy writ at the head of his homily, and comes like an equally clinching quotation at the end. A homily unanswerable, truly, by younger men, for they certainly have *not* lived as long as he has, and it *may* be owing to their getting up two hours later. Larks seem to be a special interposition of Providence in favour of these sticklers for early rising; and perhaps, though with more hesitation, we should be forced to concede the rising and setting of the sun as another. Poets, lying in bed, have sung the glories of the sunrise and the matins of the lark,—the better, perhaps, from their trusting chiefly to their fancies,—and have felt, doubtless from some mystic sympathy such as poets only know, a shrinkingly thrilling sensation in the region of the left clavicle, as they thought of this feathered exemplar's " little bill," which he presents with such assiduity at the door of his great debtor, the sun, ere he has had a chance to slip out of a morning.

The thought—as one composes his pillow for that Circean " second nap,"—that he will be called perhaps just as he is entering the sweet palace of dreams, is the

" Just clay enough to keep one down to earth,"

—the slave in the triumphal chariot to nudge and say, " Philip, thou art a man." This never takes one atom from our joy. Even if we be-

lieved it, the very fact of our being mortal adds
zest and glory to the otherwise prosaic and
everyday fact of our possessing the enjoyments
of a god. It is like the beautiful Lamia em-
bracing her mortal lover. But the cold, bare
fact that, after being called, we *must* get up, is
as if the Lamia were a serpent again, and
crushing one with her ever-tightening, scaly,
and loathsome folds. Alnaschar, when he
had kicked over his basket; Aladdin, when he
had lost his lamp; Christopher Sly, when he
woke from dukedom to tinkerdom; Stephano,
when he was baited from his short-lived royalty;—what was the fate of all these, to the
misery of being shaken by the shoulder out of
the gorgeous palaces and gardens of dreamland
into the ten-by-twelve of an attic? Moreover,
the personages aforesaid have the posthumous
satisfaction of becoming classical; whereas, your
dreamer is only rewarded by learning that the
coffee is cold, and that Betty has been in three
times to clear the breakfast table, and flounced
out, shutting the door behind her with a gradually increasing and ominous slam.

Rip van Winkle is surely entitled to our commiseration, and receives it, for *not* finding his family when he descended to breakfast from his world-attic in Catskill mountain; but methinks such suffering were light to his who finds a mother, a sister, or even a wife, only needing the overturn of his coffee on the clean table-cloth to become vocal in consolatory "oh-never-minds"—a reversed-telescope species of reproach, which puts one's ease at a yet greater distance. In a family, too, where there chances to be an old-fashioned eight-day clock, garrulous with age, which maliciously and with a devilish pertinacity, lingers out its tale of passing time till its last notes make the nervous and conscience-quickened drums of one's ears feel like what a sick man conceives of Columbian artillery bass drums on a muster day, there is no corner round which one's remorse can dodge the seemingly unconscious maternal exclamation of " Why, I declare, it 's nine o'clock ! "

It may perchance give some of your readers, Mr. Editor, a melancholy pleasure,—something like what one would fancy a capital convict might enjoy in reading a last dying speech and confession,—to hear some of my pitiful experiences.

I am just listening to a recitation, from the " rapt one of the godlike forehead," of those portions of the immortal poem of Kubla Khan which were lost to the world by the entrance of that most unhappy " visitor from Porlock,' whose name, in mercy to his descendants, has been withheld from us. Chaucer, Shakespeare, Spenser, Chapman, Fletcher, Milton, Wordsworth, and other glorious spirits, with a feet-on-the-fender expression of countenance, sit around smoking chibouks such as were never seen but in fairyland, or what " the Marchioness" rightly deemed the next place to it,—the shop windows. Princeps editions of the divinest authors, picked up at impossible book-stalls for impossible " mere songs," are ranged in gothic black oak cases round the room. In short, it is as true a " palace of pleasure " as ever Painter's was. Just as Coleridge's voice pauses, like a bee over a flower, ere it drops into a verse which all feel prophetically is to be such as only he could have conceived, there comes a rap at the door. Who can it be? Chaucer and Milton express a hope that it may be Dante or Keats. Or it may be Shelley, his fair hair glittering with the salt tears of the Adriatic; or the genial Carlyle, or Emerson, or he who was "born in a golden clime with golden stars above." It was none of these, reader,—it was my father.

My father is a most excellent man. I respect him, and I respect his opinions as much as most young men do those of sexagenarian fathers. Youths of twenty and thereabouts will appreciate the justness of the remark, when I say that parents are the most unreasonable of beings; or, as I have heard it better expressed, "our age is remarkable for its disobedient parents." But even with this in view, can you conceive what my father had to do in an assembly like this?— he, who in poetry kisses the toe of Alexander Pope, and wishes (classing them all under the name of Germans, his bitterest term of reproach,) that Wordsworth and Coleridge and Shelley, and especially Carlyle and Emerson, were— anywhere but where they are;—what, I say,

had he to do in such an assembly ? Oh, sudden
plunge from the Icarian pinions of the ideal into
the cold, salt sea of everyday life ! His errand
was—(shall I say it ?) to tell me that breakfast
was ready. I looked around timidly to note the
effect of this infaust interruption on the faces of
my companions, but they were gone, all gone
into a world of light, and I alone lay lingering
there in my own prosaic chamber.

I have always thought Brutus an unnatural
father,—first, because he had most decidedly
that appearance in the wood-cut to the two-inch
square Roman History which first introduced
my childhood to the character and manners of
classic times, he being there represented with a
most diabolical expression of feature and a
dress unbecoming even a pagan ; and secondly,
because I was doomed to read and re-read the
story for a stated time in Latin. But what was
this father to mine ? Thus to expose me as a
mere man of coffee and buttered toast in an assembly like that ! I can pardon anything sooner
than bad taste. Nay, I can forgive my friend
who indulges in a cavalier head of hair, or a

pilgrim-father chin of beard; indeed, had my
hair curled, or luxuriance followed the too easy
reaping of my razor, I might have descended to
such eccentricities myself.   But the taste that
could turn from that wondrous damsel with a
dulcimer and a feast of honey-dew and paradise-
milk to——Here my eye became fastened on a
very remarkable combination of cracks on the
ceiling which were, I was sure, extremely like
some countenance familiar to me, though I
could not think whose.   While I was yet striving to untie this Gordian knot, it was suddenly
cut, and that in a most surprising manner.   The
head took to itself a body and legs, and advanced
towards me.   It was no other than that whim-
sical German, Hoffmann, with whom I had a
slight acquaintance.   He saluted me cordially,
at the same time saying in very good English:

"Will you smoke ?   I have nothing better to
offer you than a cheroot, but I assure you they
are quite passable.   They were a present to my
friend, the Herr Archivarius Lindhorst, from
his cousin the Grand Llama; and Confucius
told me, a day or two since, that Hermes Tris-

megistus could endure no other kind of segar.
These were found by Captain Kyd, in the sar-
cophagus of Psammiticus III, a lineal descend-
ant of Nebuchadnezzar,—the report of whose
eating grass is only an ignorant scandal arising
from his being in advance of his age in a taste
for salads; though he did, in the opinion of some
uneducated minds, put too much oil—"

" Thank you," I replied, willing to interrupt
a discourse of which, though historically curious,
I saw no end ; " I will smoke one with
pleasure."

I then lighted my segar, which was truly
delicious, having in its ashes what my friend
Frank Carlisle calls " the indescribable but
almost universally undeceptive tint of mingling
snow and sunset." Looking about me as I
allowed the smoke to curl, graceful as a dancing
houri, from my placid mouth, I discovered that
I was in no less a place than Auerbach's cellar.
So then, my meeting with Coleridge and the
rest was only a dream, after all ; and my father
(thank Heaven !) is innocent, and in no wise
resembles the wood-cut of Brutus above men-

tioned. This raised my spirits, and when
Mephistopheles, at Hoffman's request, twirled
his gimblet into the oaken table and drew me
therefrom a Venice glass of Johannisberger, I
was enabled to enjoy its flavour with some com-
posure.

" The old humbug ! " cried a sneering voice
behind me, " he let the critics with infinite
labour dig up a hidden treasure of meaning from
his writings, and then stepped gravely forward
and claimed it all as owner of the soil. If the
moon had been green cheese, he would have
been disobliging enough to find it out and nudge
us to tell us of it, just as we were reading
Endymion, or Lorenzo and Jessica ! "

"That is Henry Heine," said my friend; "he
is speaking of the Olympian Goethe."

" See what a Walpurgis-night-dance our
shadows———"

" Am I then discovered ? " shrieked a tall
young man in black, springing up and rushing
from the room.

" Is he crazy ? " said I.

" No," answered a man whom I recognized

as Ahasuerus, the Wandering Jew, "'t is only Peter Schlemihl, poor fellow. If he only had a shadow, he would look very much like his ancestor, Peter the Less, who, I remember——"

Here a little man at the next table looked over his spectacles and exclaimed, "Remember! pray, how could you remember him? Why, let me see, he died in the year of our Lord——"

"The devil!" groaned Ahasuerus, leaping through the window.

"Twelve hundred and ten," finished the little man, resuming his pipe gravely without noticing the interruption.

"The man whose delicacy does not hinder him from wantonly injuring the sensibilities of others, deserves to have his own in turn disregarded," said Dr. Johnson, whom I had not before noticed, at the same time casting a sneering and severe glance at a mulberry coat which adorned the person of Goldsmith, who sat next him. Charles Dickens, who had somehow mixed up his personal identity with that of Boswell, carefully entered the remark in his notebook.

I now for the first time observed a small man seated at a piano in one corner, and moving his fingers over the keys with the wildest enthusiasm. His whole soul seemed to leap down upon the instrument like a tiger on its prey. Such melodies I never heard. Now a huge column of music would slowly raise itself like a great waterspout from the foaming sea beneath, and then burst in a cataract of sparkling notes. Sometimes I thought I saw a single golden bird soaring and singing through the blue air, and then suddenly all would be dark, and I could hear the trampling of an innumerable host, with shouts and torches flaring in the melancholy night-wind. Then a beam of sunshine like a silver spear would pierce through the solid gloom, and I saw mossy dells and streams all green with overhanging leaves where the first violets were glassing themselves.

I saw the meadows where I played in boyhood,—I saw flowers such as I seem never to have seen since those blue, sunny days, and I held in my hand again one of the rude little May-day nosegays which I was wont to tie

together with a long grassblade and surprise my
mother with. Ah, what a smell of childhood
and spring and freshness there was in everything ! Sometimes the notes seemed to linger
as if they enjoyed their own sweetness, and then
suddenly they would leap away like a chirping
flight of grasshoppers.

I always have loved the organ, because it
seemed to have more depth and majestic vast-
ness than other instruments ; and often, when I
am listening to the silvery notes of the orchestra
at a concert, I have wished that the great organ
behind would burst forth, without the touch of
any hand, and drown all other sounds in its
heaving sea of harmony.   But when I hear the
organ, I long for the ocean as yet more vast
and majestic.   But in the great soul and spirit
of this music, even in its gentlest tones, I felt
that ocean was mean and small.   As I listened,
I cannot tell what I saw and heard.   It was
Beethoven.

Milton, who stood near him, with a serene
and kingly countenance, turned his face toward
him and said,

" Would I could give thee back thine ears as thou hast given me mine eyes ! "

" Nay," answered Beethoven, " my deafness indeed shuts out from me the noises of this world, but only that I may forehear the harmonies of the next."

" Do you call *that* music ? " said Russell, ' the vocalist ' ; " why, I heard nothing,—the piano has no strings."

" That part of music which we cannot hear, is the true music ; even as that part of Nature which we cannot see, is the true Nature, and that part of poetry which the poet could not write, the true poetry," a voice said.

" Fiddlestick ! " muttered Pope and growled Johnson in a breath.

" I am always noble when I hear such music," said one.

" He who does not inwardly create such music by a true, harmonious life, cannot be noble," replied the voice. It was a woman's,—I knew not whose.

At this moment a knight in complete armour entered, and, introducing himself as the Baron

Huldbrand, invited me to spend a few days at his castle on the Danube. The hope of seeing Undine was enough, and in five minutes I was on the back of a snow-white Arabian, with a motion like a wave, and a tail like a silver water-fall. I had just a consciousness of sweeping by the Black Huntsman on the Hartz mountains, though he spurred hotly to keep pace with us,— when the Baron blew his horn, the drawbridge was lowered, and our horses' hoofs clattered on the stone pavement of the court-yard.

The porter was no less a personage than Caleb Balderstone, and strikingly resembled Sir Walter Scott. Indeed, I might have mistaken him for that great man had I not read his death in the papers the day before. In another moment Undine was in her husband's arms. Her connection with the Water-Spirits was evident in the tones of her voice, which sounded like a brook gurgling over mossy stones under a murmurous pine-tree. It threw me into a delicious reverie, and in fancy I was at home in my New-England woods again, when I was summoned to dinner. I was carving a slice from a large roasted wild-boar, when the same little man who had driven Ahasuerus from Auerbach's, and who was Gifford, the editor of the Quarterly, looked up at me and said in a sandy-haired tone of voice,

"I will take a piece not quite so fat, I thank you."

How he came there I could not divine; but I had the carving-knife in my hand and the thought of poor Keats in my heart. I made a spring at him and seized him by the hair, but he eluded me, leaving his wig in my grasp. I however caught him near an open window over the court-yard. There I deliberately cut his head from his body, (after turning the edge of my knife in an ineffectual attempt to pierce his heart,) and threw it out of the window. It alighted on the head of another critic below, and, displacing it, fixed itself firmly in its stead without his seeming conscious of the change. This gentleman has since very much distinguished himself as an enemy of the new school of philosophy and poetry. Almost before I was aware of what I had done, I was in Newgate, having been tried, damned, and sentenced, in the interim, by Lord Thurlow.

The morning of my execution was bitter cold; but, in spite of this, all round the scaffold surged and tossed a sea of horrid faces, none of whose features my dizzy eyes could discern. The chaplain told me to pray, and I repeated "Now I lay me down to sleep," being the only prayer I could in my bewilderment recollect. The hangman, who was the very conservative Mr. Dennis, immortalized in Barnaby Rudge, was drumming with his feet upon the scaffold to warm them, and muttering something about kept waiting till his breakfast was cold. One by one the cannibals below took up the cry, and yelled and screamed the same words over and over, till they grew absolutely horrible. But above all I could hear Mr. Dennis's feet drumming, and his infernal muttering about his breakfast,—and I awoke to hear my father knocking a second time at my door, and telling me in a remonstrating tone that they had taken breakfast an hour ago, and that mine was irretrievably cooled.

Disquisition on Foreheads

By Job Simikins

"O, Altitudo!"
—Sir Thomas Browne

"Such is the iniquity of men that they suck in opinions as wild asses do the wind."
—Bishop Taylor

THE humorous Charles Lamb divides the human species into two distinct races: "the men who borrow, and the men who lend." This division lacks *definiteness;* for these races too often become intermingled. We choose to divide the species into *men with high and men with low foreheads.* If it be objected to this, that there are some who have foreheads which are neither high or low, but intermediate,—like Washington's for instance,—we reply that such must be considered either as not belonging to the human species, or else as amphibious animals, having some qualities peculiar to both and each of these races.

Those belonging to the high forehead race, strikingly resemble, in some particulars, Lamb's great race of borrowers. "Their infinite superiority is discernible in their figure, port, and a certain instinctive air of sovereignty. What a careless, even deportment they have! What rosy gills!" With what perfect self-complacency he of the high forehead visiteth his looking-glass, and halteth thereat; brushing away and plastering down with brush and Macassar

each envious hair that offereth to obscure any
portion of that expanded arc of bald cuticle !
With what condescension he looketh down upon
his brethren of the inferior race ! And verily
he hath reason; for the world backs up his pretensions, and maintains that a high forehead is
not only prima facie, but almost incontrovertible,
evidence of superiority of intellect; and that
with a *low* one, a man must be little better than
" non compos," or else a strange exception to
nature's law.

But.of all the absurd opinions of the world,
this is the climax. For it is neither more nor
less than saying that a man's mind depends on
the quantity of his *hair*, or on the size of his
scalp. Allowing this be true, he who is bald to
the occipital bone, will possess at least twice the
intellect of people in general; and if his head be
bald as a ninepin ball to the *cerebellum*, he will
be a greater genius than has yet afflicted our
globe. On this theory, a fool may be metamor-
phosed instanter into a genius, by sending him
on a single campaign against the Seminoles; or
if such a journey be deemed too expensive, or if

its tendency would be to "*put him back*" at all, he could easily take the measure of the forehead or the scalp of any great man, and *shave up* to any amount of intellect which is requisite to satisfy his ambition. We wonder that the quacks who vend bottled drugs for " eradicating superfluous hair," find so few patients. It must be because, after all, men do not entirely believe the doctrine.

The origin of the world's absurd opinion respecting foreheads, has by some been ascribed to the influence of Lavater and his execrable book. It is true this may have had some influence in deepening preëxisting impressions. It is very certain that those who scout Lavater's theory on all other points, still hold to him in this; and though they now confess that they do not fully believe that a man's *courage* lies in the *bridge of his nose*, or that his *memory* depends on the shape of his eyebrows, they do yet hold that his intellect depends on the height of his forehead; and consequently that the more hair an individual has on his head, the greater fool is he. Each of the capillæ subtracts something

from the brain; because the *sap*, which would
otherwise go to form *brain*, is necessarily drawn
off to support the growth of mere useless *hair*.
This theory, we must confess, is clear and
philosophical.

We think Lavater cannot fairly be entitled
to the honour of this sublime discovery in animal science. The ancients, though they never
had the impudence to assert directly what he
has done, nevertheless talk of majestic and noble
brows, (meaning *high* ones, probably,) as if they
were necessary to make up a perfect man or
deity. But our modern romancers carry the
theory to far greater perfection than the ancients,
or the philosopher himself. Not only their
heroes, but all their respectable characters are
endowed with the highest sort of foreheads;
whereas, a *low* forehead, in their descriptions, is
a sure antitype of coming meanness, treachery,
and rascality. This holds, however, only in
their descriptions of *men*, or rather their *caricatures* of men;—for knowing as they do, that all
women have *low* foreheads, except those who are
remarkably stupid or vicious, they express the

meanness of *female* character by certain names; and so Peggy, Abigail, Betsey, &c., have become synonyms for unprincipled go-betweens and idiotic femmes de chambre.

A fellow calling himself *William Shakespeare* (a playwright, who lived, we believe, in the sixteenth century, or thereabouts, and of whom some few of our readers may possibly have heard), talks in one place of a person having a " villainous low forehead "; thus deliberately coupling *villainy* with a low forehead. But to show the true cause of this calumnious expression, it will only be necessary to inform our readers that this Shakespeare had a remarkably bald head of his own, or in other words a very high forehead, to which he was desirous of calling people's attention. The use of this expression, then, was only evidence of his gross vanity. It was as much as to say, " Look at *my* forehead ! See how mighty intellect and noble heart protrude from under my *small scalp !* " Had he inherited a scalp which came down within a short inch of his proboscis, would he, think you, have used that abominable expression ? Self-love shudders at the thought. But all *others* who have praised high foreheads and vilified *low* ones, will be found to have been men who wore their foreheads *high*, so that this praise and vilification are naught but sheer egotism. *Decent* men do not praise what they actually possess, but only such things as they need and desire. He who praises what he possesses, sets himself above those who are lacking in that thing, thereby proving his own arrogant vanity. Now you never know of a man who had one of these villainous low foreheads expressing these contemptuous and contemptible opinions of low foreheads, or putting any great value upon high ones; so that it is only the high forehead gentry who praise or value them at all. Argal, we argue justly that the possession of a high forehead may prove a man to be a self-conceited, self-eulogizing coxcomb; but it goes not one step toward proving him to be an intelligent man.

But these coxcombs tell us sneeringly that ourang outangs, apes, and monkeys, have low foreheads; some of the smartest of them even go so far as to call *low* foreheads "*monkey* foreheads "; meaning by that disgraceful metaphor to insinuate that men with low foreheads are very nearly assimilated to the simian tribe. Now to answer this malicious innuendo in a becoming manner requires some consideration. The low forehead race are universally modest, meek, forbearing, and nonresistant, though of noble and generous hearts. When they are reviled, they revile not again; it is contrary to their principles to *retort* in any manner. If it were not for this, we might reply, and justly too, that the monkey tribe, considering their very limited advantages of education, manifest *much greater* sagacity and intelligence than the majority of the high forehead race; their countenances, too, are vastly *more* expressive,—the beaming of their eyes is much *more* brilliant and intellectual; in fact, excepting the high forehead, they have all Lavater's requisites of great geniuses,—and undoubtedly they are so, but their condition has always been so *depressed*, that they have never yet been able to prove themselves so much superior to the high forehead race as they undoubtedly would under a more impartial system of *free schools*, where they might fairly try their strength together.

We say we *might* retort in this manner, but we scorn to retort at all; and would only meekly request these revilers to inquire of any menagerie-keeper, if it be not true that those monkeys, &c., which have the *lowest* foreheads are decidedly the more sagacious and intelligent. They will then learn something which will startle their self-conceit not a little.

But I beg those who are still inclined to sneer at the low forehead race, to remember that they sneer at the memory of such men as Fisher Ames, General Knox, and John Jay*, whom we mention as being our own countrymen; and at such living men as Dr. Beecher, John C. Calhoun, and Father Taylor, and hundreds of distinguished men, to name whom it is not convenient, just now, to tax my memory. The reason why *all* the distinguished men are not of this race is, that the vast majority of mankind are of the *high* forehead race, and *out-vote* the minority; and that " the vast majority of man-

* Vide " Familiar Letters"

kind are fools," is a fact which some one discovered long ago. *I* glory in belonging to the
smaller and nobler portion of mankind. I consider it really a glorious and honourable distinction, a precious privilege, to be allowed to wear
my forehead low. This distinction and privilege is as honourable as that of being called
Mister, in these days when everybody is a colonel,
judge, or 'squire. Find a man without a title,
now-a-days, and you are sure to find an unas-
suming, but a thinking, intellectual man. Your
brazen-faced fellows who have high foreheads
and no brains, monopolize all the titles.

But we should grossly libel the high forehead
race were we to assert and maintain that they
were all *brazen*-faced, and therefore we hasten
to correct any false impression made by the last
sentence. You will never find a peculiarly
owl-faced, *sheepish*-looking, *leaden*-eyed fellow,
but he glories in a high forehead, and rests his
pretensions to intellect (*very properly*) on that
fact. The longer I live and the more I observe,
the more clear does this truth become. But
under each of those long despised *monkey* fore-

heads, you will not fail to see a couple of orbs radiant with intelligence ; unless, indeed, there is *but one left*, as is, alas! too often the case. But even then you shall see the sole star light up and flash (whenever and wherever the fire of eloquence, argument, and wit is going on the hottest), like the remaining cylinder of a double-barrelled gun, after its fellow is burst and gone. The majority (in one part of America, at least,) of that noble order, the I. O. O. F., are the low forehead race ; and I might challenge the world to find a class of wiser, nobler, or more benevolent men. *Some* of the *high* forehead race obtain admittance there, but they are " raræ aves,"—exceptions to the mass out of which they are taken.

" Villainous low foreheads," quoth Shakespeare ! I never think of the expression without a blush on account of the egregious vanity of that rank libeller. Out upon the opprobrious epithet ! There is not the smallest infinitesimal of truth in it. On the contrary, there is every reason to believe that " villainous *high* foreheads " would be much nearer the truth, for

Cain was the first murderer and first villain, and
that he was the great progenitor of the *high*
forehead race will be acknowledged on a single
moment's reflection. The bible tells us that a
mark was set upon him, lest any finding him
should kill him. Now all men, even to the
sceptical Byron, acknowledge that the mark
was put upon his forehead,—and why ? Plainly
because that was the most conspicuous place.
But if his forehead had been a " *monkey* " forehead, the mark could not have been readily seen,
and so the object of it might have failed at any
time. Hence, all will allow that it is reasonable
to conclude that instead of a villainous *low* forehead, Cain had a villainous and remarkably *high*
one.

But the proof is equally clear that *Adam* was
of the *low* forehead race. The curse reads:
" in the sweat of thy *face* (not brow) shalt thou
eat bread." The world often quotes the text
incorrectly by following the wicked perversion
of one *John Milton*, who was himself of the
high forehead, race. The object of that perversion is too clearly manifest to need any com-

ment of mine. Had Adam really had a *high* forehead, Milton's expression would have been the *bible* expression, because the brow would then have constituted a very large portion of the face, and the part on which perspiration would first appear; the expression, too, would have been more *elegant*. But the fact that Milton's expression is *not* the bible expression, proves conclusively that Adam had very little forehead, if any at all.

The strong prejudice which has existed against low foreheads, ever since the fall of man and his consequent total depravity, has often led painters and sculptors to *flatter* their subjects, as they thought, by conferring high foreheads. And at this day, let one of the low forehead race sit for his portrait, and he will be astonished to find how much higher his forehead appears on canvas than it is in reality. But as chairman of the committee to whom this subject has been confided, I hereby publish to all painters that we are henceforth determined to repudiate all such *flattered* likenesses, for it is such flattery as we cannot appreciate; but we promise said painters that if they will *shorten* our forehead, so that the edge of the hair may seem to be gently resting upon, or commingling with the eyebrows, like a thunder-cloud settling upon the dark mountains, we will pay them a fair per centage for their trouble.

But not only painters but biographers manifest the same ludicrous prejudices, and think it necessary to apologize for, or palliate, their hero's low forehead, much as if it were the vice of gambling or intemperance. Now, had these apologists only taken the pains to ask the hero, in his life-time, how he would desire that trouble to be disposed of, he would have replied in language peculiar to the noble race of low foreheads :

" Tell the world that my forehead was both low and narrow, and that I gloried in the fact, for I consider that and that only a sure physiognomical proof of superior intellect ; although I never had the vanity or arrogance to boast of it in public."

I have said that our race is modest, meek, and forbearing. Hence it is that we can so calmly

read the cart-loads of trashy novels to which we
have already alluded, and reply to all their petty
insinuations and libellous caricatures with only
a mild and uncle-Toby-like smile of self-complacency. We are *still* willing that these ambitious witlings should load the press and overrun
the world with fictitious heroes, dressed up with
foreheads *which are the exact facsimiles of the
writer's own;* we only laugh at all this. Hitherto
we have, in the glorious consciousness of our
own rectitude and soundness of mind, calmly
borne taunts the most malicious, sneers the
most contemptible, content by an eloquent
silence to hurl them back into the very throat
of their authors, by quietly suffering, in Shakespeare's own *self-condemning* words,

> . . . the scoffs
> Which patient merit of the unworthy takes.

How much longer our patience will hold out
we cannot say. But we beg people to remember that, somewhere in dim futurity, there may
be " a point where forbearance ceases to be a
virtue." You may poke the slumbering lion
too often! Let no one undertake to predict

the dire results of the contest, when our rage shall be at last aroused, and high forehead and low forehead meet in dreadful war of extermination. Nothing to it has been the long waged battle of the big *wigs*. We are told that the very hairs of our heads are all numbered ; and in that day each one, still looking out valiantly for number one, shall glance with jealous eye upon the numbers of his neighbours. We ardently hope that this unnatural combat may be long postponed, but we of the low foreheads are prepared for it when it must come. We glory in this " head and front of our offending," and cannot long submit to be *browbeat* as we have been. Let then our antagonists contract their brows in their fear of our wrath, and prepare to " hide their diminished heads," remembering that when it comes to " heaping coals of fire," we have the advantage.

Song-Writing

From this to that, from that to
  this he flies,
Feels music's pulse in all her
  arteries.

With flash of high-born fancies,
  here and there
Dancing in lofty measures, and
  anon
Creeps on the soft touch of a
  tender tone,
Whose   trembling murmurs,
  melting in wild airs,
Run to and fro complaining their
  sweet cares;
Because those precious mysteries that dwell
In music's ravished soul he
  dare not tell,
But whisper to the world.

    Crashawe (from Strada)

THE songs of a nation are like wild flowers pressed, as it were by chance, between the blood-stained pages of history. As if a man's heart had paused for a moment in its dusty march, and looked back with a flutter of the pulse and a tearful smile upon the simple peacefulness of happier and purer days, gathering some wayside blossom to remind it of childhood and home, amid the crash of battle or the din of the market. Listening to these strains of pastoral music, we are lured away from the records of patriotic frauds, of a cannibal policy which devours whole nations with the refined appetite of a converted and polished Polyphemus who has learned to eat with a silver fork, and never to put his knife in his mouth,—we forget the wars and the false standards of honour which have cheated men into wearing the fratricidal brand of Cain, as if it were but the glorious trace of a dignifying wreath, and hear the rustle of the leaves and the innocent bleat of lambs, and the low murmur of lovers beneath the moon of

Arcady, or the long twilight of the north. The earth grows green again, and flowers spring up in the scorching footprints of Alaric, but where love hath but only smiled, some gentle trace of it remains freshly for ever. The infinite sends its messages to us by untutored spirits, and the lips of little children, and the unboastful beauty of simple nature; not with the sound of trumpet, and the tramp of mail-clad hosts. Simplicity and commonness are the proofs of Beauty's divinity. Earnestly and beautifully touching is this eternity of simple feeling from age to age,—this trustfulness with which the heart flings forth to the wind its sybilline leaves to be gathered and cherished as oracles for ever. The unwieldy current of life whirls and writhes and struggles muddily onward, and there in mid-current the snow-white lilies blow in un-stained safety, generation after generation. The cloud-capt monuments of mighty kings and captains crumble into dust and mingle with the nameless ashes of those who reared them; but we know perhaps the name and even the

colour of the hair and eyes of some humble shep-
herd's mistress who brushed through the dew
to meet her lover's kiss, when the rising sun
glittered on the golden images that crowned the
palace-roof of Semiramis. Fleets and navies
are overwhelmed and forgotten, but some tiny
love-freighted argosy, launched (like those of
the Hindoo maidens) upon the stream of time in
days now behind the horizon, floats down to us
with its frail lamp yet burning. Theories for
which great philosophers wore their hearts out,
histories over which the eyes of wise men ached for
weary years, creeds for which hundreds underwent
an exulting martyrdom, poems which had once
quickened the beating of the world's great heart,
and the certainty of whose deathlessness had
made death sweet to the poet,—all these have
mouldered to nothing; but some word of love,
some outvent of a sorrow which haply filled only
one pair of eyes with tears, these seem to have
become a part of earth's very life-blood. They
live because those who wrote never thought
whether they would live or not. Because they

were the children of human nature, human nature has tenderly fostered them, while children only begot to perpetuate the foolish vanity of their father's name must trust for their support to such inheritance of livelihood as their father left them. There are no pensions and no retired lists in the pure democracy of nature and truth.

A good song is as if the poet had pressed his heart against the paper, and that could have conveyed its hot, tumultuous throbbings to the reader. The low, musical rustle of the wind among the leaves is song-like, but the slow unfolding of the leaves and blossoms, and under them the conception and ripening of the golden fruit through long summer days of sunshine and of rain, are like the grander, but not more beautiful or eternal offspring of poesy. The song-writer must take his place somewhere between the poet and the musician, and must form a distinct class by himself. The faculty of writing songs is certainly a peculiar one, and as perfect in its kind as that of writing epics. They can

only be written by true poets ; like the mistle-
toe, they are slender and delicate, but they only
grow in oaks. Burns is as wholly a poet, but
not as great a poet, as Milton. Songs relate to
us the experience and hoarded learning of the
feelings, greater poems detail that of the mind.
One is the result of that wisdom which the
heart keeps by remaining young, the other of
that which it gains by growing old. Songs are
like inspired nursery-rhymes, which make the
soul childlike again. The best songs have always some tinge of a mysterious sadness in
them. They seem written in the night-watches
of the heart, and reflect the spiritual moonlight,
or the shifting flashes of the northern-light, or
the trembling lustre of the stars, rather than the
broad and cheerful benediction of the sunny
day. Often they are the merest breaths, vague
snatches of half-heard music which fell dreamily
on the ear of the poet while he was listening
for grander melodies, and which he hummed
over afterward to himself, not knowing how or
where he learned them.

A true song touches no feeling or prejudice of education, but only the simple, original elements of our common nature. And perhaps the mission of the song-writer may herein be deemed loftier and diviner than any other, since he sheds delight over more hearts, and opens more rude natures to the advances of civilization, refinement, and a softened humanity, by revealing to them a beauty in their own simple thoughts and feelings which wins them unconsciously to a dignified reverence for their own noble capabilities as men. He who aspires to the highest triumphs of the muse, must look at first for appreciation and sympathy only from a few, and must wait till the progress of education shall have enlarged the number and quickened the sensibility and apprehension of his readers. But the song-writer finds his ready welcome in those homespun, untutored artistic perceptions which are the birthright of every human soul, and which are the sure pledges of the coming greatness and ennoblement of the race. He makes men's hearts ready to receive the teachings of his nobler brother. He is not positively, but only relatively, a greater blessing to his kind, since, in God's good season, by the sure advance of freedom, all men shall be able to enjoy what is now the privilege of the few, and Shakespeare and Milton shall be as dear to the heart of the cottager and the craftsman as Burns or Beranger. Full of grandeur, then, and yet fuller of awful responsibility, is the calling of the song-writer. It is no wild fancy to deem that he may shape the destiny of coming ages. Like an electric spark, his musical thought flits glittering from heart to heart and from lip to lip through the land. Luther's noble hymns made more and truer protestants than ever did his sermons or his tracts. The song hummed by some toiling mother to beguile the long monotony of the spinning wheel may have turned the current of her child's thoughts as he played about her knee, and given the world a hero or apostle. We know not when or in what soil God may plant the seeds of our spiritual enlightenment and regeneration, but we may be sure that it will be in some piece of clay common to all mankind, some heart whose simple feelings call the whole world kin. Not from mighty poet or deep-seeking philosopher will come the word which all men long to hear, but in the lowly Nazareth of some unlearned soul, in the rough manger of rudest, humblest sympathies, shall the true Messiah be born and cradled. In the inspired heart, not in the philosophic intellect, all true reforms originate, and it is over this that the songwriter has unbridled sway. He concentrates the inarticulate murmur and longing of a trampled people into the lightning-flash of a fiery verse, and, ere the guilty heart of the oppressor has ceased to flutter, follows the deafening thunderclap of revolution. He gives vent to his love of a flower or a maiden, and adds so much to the store of every-day romance in the heart of the world, refining men's crude perceptions of beauty and dignifying their sweet natural affections. Once it was the fashion to write pastorals, but he teaches us that it is not nature to make all men talk like rustics, but

rather to show that one heart beats under homespun and broadcloth, and that it alone is truly
classical, and gives eternity to verse.

Songs are scarcely amenable to the common
laws of criticism. If anything were needed to
prove the utter foolishness of the assertion that
that only is good poetry which can be reduced
to good prose, we might summon as witnesses
the most perfect songs in our language. The
best part of a song lies often not at all in the
words, but in the metre, perhaps, or the structure of the verse, in the wonderful melody
which arose of itself from the feeling of the
writer, and which unawares throws the heart
into the same frame of thought. Ben Jonson
was used to write his poems first in prose, and
then translate or distil them into verse, and had
we not known the fact, we might have almost
guessed it from reading some of his lyrics, the
mechanical structure of whose verse is as different from the spontaneous growth of a true song
(which must be written one way or not at all)
as a paper flower is from a violet. In a good
song the words seem to have given birth to the

melody, and the melody to the words. The strain of music seems to have wandered into the poet's heart, and to have been the thread round which his thoughts have crystallized. There is always something of personal interest in songs. They are the true diary of the poet's spiritual life, the table-talk of his heart. There is nothing egoistical in them, for the inward history of a poet is never a commonplace one, and egoism can only be a trait of little minds, its disagreeable quality lying wholly in this, that it constantly thrusts in our faces the egoist's individuality, which is really the least noticeable thing about him. We love to hear wonderful men talk of themselves, because they are better worth hearing about than anything else, and because what we learn of them is not so much a history of self as a history of nature, and a statement of facts therein which are so many finger-posts to set us right in our search after true spiritual knowledge. Songs are translations from the language of the spiritual into that of the natural world.

As love is the highest and holiest of all
feelings, so those songs are best in which love
is the essence. All poetry must rest on love
for a foundation, or it will only last so long
as the bad passions it appeals to, and which
it is the end of true poesy to root out. If there
be not in it a love of man, there must at
least be a love of nature, which lies next below it, and which, as is the nature of all
beauty, will lead its convert upward to that
nobler and wider sympathy. True poetry is
but the perfect reflex of true knowledge, and
true knowledge is spiritual knowledge, which
comes only of love, and which, when it has
solved the mystery of one, even the smallest
effluence of the eternal beauty, which surrounds
us like an atmosphere, becomes a clue leading
to the heart of the seeming labyrinth. All our
sympathies lie in such close neighbourhood, that
when music is drawn from one string all the
rest vibrate in sweet accord. As in the womb
the brain of the child changes, with a steady
rise, through a likeness to that of one animal and
another, till it is perfected in that of man, the

highest animal, so in this life, which is but as a womb wherein we are shaping to be born in the next, we are led upward from love to love till we arrive at the love of God, which is the highest love. Many things unseal the springs of tenderness in us ere the full glory of our nature gushes forth to the one benign spirit which interprets for us all mystery, and is the key to unlock all the most secret shrines of beauty. Woman was given us to love chiefly to this end, that the sereneness and strength which the soul wins from that full sympathy with one, might teach it the more divine excellence of a sympathy with all, and that it was man's heart only which God shaped in His own image, which it can only rightly emblem in an all-surrounding love. Therefore, we put first those songs which tell of love, since we see in them not an outpouring of selfish and solitary passion, but an indication of that beautiful instinct which prompts the heart of every man to turn towards its fellows with a smile, and to recognize its master even in the disguise of clay; and we confess that the sight of the rudest and simplest love-verses in the corner of a village newspaper oftener bring tears of delight into our eyes than awaken a sense of the ludicrous. In fancy we see the rustic lovers wandering hand in hand, a sweet fashion not yet extinct in our quiet New England villages, and crowding all the past and future with the blithe sunshine of the present. The modest loveliness of Dorcas has revealed to the delighted heart of Reuben countless other beauties, of which, but for her, he had been careless. Pure and delicate sympathies have overgrown protectingly the most exposed part of his nature, as the moss covers the north side of the tree. The perception and reverence of her beauty has become a new and more sensitive conscience to him, which, like the wonderful ring in the fairy tale, warns him against every danger that may assail his innocent self-respect. For the first time he begins to see something more in the sunset than an omen of to-morrow's weather. The flowers, too, have grown tenderly dear to him of a sudden, and, as he plucks a sprig of blue succory from the roadside to deck her hair with, he is as truly a poet as Burns, when he embalmed the

" mountain daisy " in deathless rhyme. Dorcas
thrills at sight of quivering Hesperus as keenly as
ever Sappho did, and, as it brings back to her,
she knows not how, the memory of all happy
times in one, she clasps closer the brown, toil-
hardened hand which she holds in hers, and
which the heart that warms it makes as soft as
down to her. She is sure that the next Sabbath
evening will be as cloudless and happy as this.
She feels no jealousy of Reuben's love of the
flowers, for she knows that only the pure in heart
can see God in them, and that they will but
teach him to love better the wild-flower-like beauties in herself, and give him impulses of kindliness
and brotherhood to all. Love is the truest
radicalism, lifting all to the same clear-aired
level of humble, thankful humanity. Dorcas
begins to think that her childish dream has
come true, and that she is really an enchanted
princess, and her milk-pans are forthwith
changed to a service of gold plate, with the
family arms engraved on the bottom of each,
the device being a great heart, and the legend,
God gives, man only takes away. Her taste in '

dress has grown wonderfully more refined since her betrothal, though she never heard of the Paris fashions, and never had more than one silk gown in her life, that one being her mother's wedding dress made over again. Reuben has grown so tender-hearted that he thought there might be some good even in " Transcendentalism," a terrible dragon of straw, against which he had seen a lecturer at the village lyceum valorously enact the St. George,—nay, he goes so far as to think that the slave women (black though they be, and therefore not deserving so much happiness) cannot be quite so well off as his sister in the factory, and would sympathize with them if the constitution did not enjoin all good citizens not to do so. But we are wandering—farewell Reuben and Dorcas! remember that you can only fulfil your vow of being true to each other by being true to all, and be sure that death can but unclasp your bodily hands that your spiritual ones may be joined the more closely.

The songs of our great poets are unspeakably precious. In them find vent those irrepressible utterances of homely fireside humanity, inconsistent with the loftier aim and self-forgetting enthusiasm of a great poem, which preserve the finer and purer sensibilities from wilting and withering under the black frost of ambition. The faint records of flitting impulses, we light upon them sometimes imbedded round the bases of the basaltic columns of the epic or the drama, like heedless insects or tender ferns which had fallen in while those gigantic crystals were slowly shaping themselves in the molten entrails of the soul all aglow with the hidden fires of inspiration, or like the tracks of birds from far-off climes, which had lighted upon the ductile mass ere it had hardened into eternal rock. They make the lives of the masters of the lyre encouragements and helps to us, by teaching us humbly to appreciate and sympathize with, as men, those whom we should else almost have worshipped as beings of a higher order. In Shakespeare's dramas we watch with awe the struggles and triumphs and defeats, which seem almost triumphs, of his unmatched soul ;—in his songs we can yet feel the beating of a simple, warm heart, the mate of which can be found under the first homespun frock you meet on the high road. He who, instead of carefully plucking the fruit from the tree of knowledge, as others are fain to, shook down whole showers of leaves and twigs and fruit at once; who tossed down systems of morality and philosophy by the handful; who wooed nature as a superior, and who carpeted the very earth beneath the delicate feet of his fancy with such flowers of poesy as bloom but once in a hundred years,—this vast and divine genius in his songs and his unequalled sonnets, (which are but epic songs, songs written, as it were, for an organ or rather ocean accompaniment,) shows all the humbleness, and wavering, and self-distrust, with which the weakness of the flesh tempers souls of the boldest aspiration and most unshaken self-help, as if to remind them gently of that brotherhood to assert and dignify whose claims they were sent forth as apostles.

We mean to copy a few of the best songs, chiefly selecting from those of English poets. To some of our readers many of our extracts will be new, and those who are familiar with them will thank us, perhaps, for threading so many pearls upon one string. We shall begin our specimens by copying the first verse of an old English song, the composition of which Warton assigns to the beginning of the thirteenth century. There seems to us to be a very beautiful and pure *animal* feeling of nature in it, and altogether a freshness and breeziness which is delightful, after sifting over the curiosæ *in*felicitates of most of the later poets. We shall alter the spelling enough to make it intelligible at a glance, and change the tense of one of the words to give it the metrical harmony of the original.

> Summer is acoming in,
> Loudly sing cuckoo !
> Groweth seed,
> And bloweth mead,
> And springeth the wood anew :
> Sing cuckoo! cuckoo!

There is something in this song to us like the smell of a violet, which has a felicity of association to bring back the May-day delights of childhood in all their innocent simpleness, and cool the feverish brow of the present by wreathing around it the dewy flowers of the past. There is a straightforward plainness in this little verse, which is one of the rarest, as it is also one of the most needful, gifts of a poet, who must have a man's head and a child's heart.

Chaucer furnishes us with no specimen of a song, which we cannot but lament, since there are verses of his, in " The Cuckoo and the Nightingale " and " The Flower and the Leaf " especially, which run over with sweetness both of sentiment and melody, and have all that delightful *unintentionalness* (if we may use the word) which is the charm and essence of a true song, in which the heart, as it were, speaks unconsciously aloud, and, like Wordsworth's stock dove, " broods over its own sweet voice." He is like one of those plants which, though they do not blossom, sprinkle their leaves with the hues which had been prepared in the sap to furnish forth the flowers.

Although Shakespeare's songs are so familiar, yet we cannot resist copying one of them, since we can nowhere find such examples as in him, who, like nature herself, is as minutely perfect in his least as in his greatest work. His songs are delicate sea-mosses cast up by chance from the deeps of that ocean-like heart in whose struggling abysses it seems a wonder that such fragile perfectness could have grown up in safety.

> Hark! hark! the lark at heaven's gate sings,
> And Phœbus 'gins arise,
> His steeds to water at those springs
> On chaliced flowers that lies;
> And winking marybuds begin
> To ope their golden eyes,
> With everything that pretty bin;
> My lady sweet, arise,
> Arise, arise!

There are some beautiful songs scattered about among Beaumont and Fletcher's plays, of which we copy one from " The Maid's Tragedy." There is a humble plaintiveness in it which is touching.

> Lay a garland on my hearse
> Of the dismal yew;
> Maidens, willow branches bear,
> Say I died true:

My love was false, but I was firm
From my hour of birth :
Upon my buried bosom lie
Lightly, gentle earth.

Ben Jonson was scarcely of fine organization
enough to write songs of the first order.   A
vein of prosaic common-sense runs quite through
him, and he seems never to have wholly forgotten his old profession of bricklaying, generally putting his thoughts together with as much
squareness and regularity as so many bricks.
It is only a blissful ignorance which presumes
that poetic souls want common-sense.   In truth,
men are poets not in proportion to their *want* of
any faculty whatsoever, but inasmuch as they are
gifted with a very *un*common sense, which enables
them always to see things purely in their relations to spirit, and not matter.   Rare Ben did
not wander musingly up Parnassus, lured onward by winding paths and flowery nooks of
green stillness, and half-glimpses of divine
shapes, the oreads of that enchanted hill, but,
having resolved to climb, he struggled manfully
up, little heeding what flowers he might crush
with his stout pedestrian shoes.   We copy two

verses from " The Masque of the Fortunate
Isles," — merely alluding to his sweet song
" To Celia," as too well known to need
quotation.

> Look forth, thou shepherd of the seas,
> And of the ports that keep'st the keys,
>   And to your Neptune tell,
> Macaria, prince of all the isles,
> Wherein there nothing grows but smiles,
>   Doth here put in to dwell.
>
> The windes are sweet, and gently blow,
> But Zephyrus, no breath they know,
>   The father of the flowers :
> By him the virgin violets live,
> And every plant doth odours give
>   As new as are the bowers.

From William Browne, a pastoral poet of
great sweetness and delicacy, we glean the
following stanzas. They are somewhat similar
to those of Jonson, copied above, but are
more purely songlike, and more poetical in
expression. Milton, perhaps, remembered the
two lines that we have italicized, when he
was writing his exquisite song in Comus, a
part of which we shall presently quote. The
verses are from the fifth song in the second
book of " Brittania's Pastorals."

Swell then, gently swell, ye floods,
As proud of what ye bear,
And nymphs that in low coral woods
String pearls upon your hair,
Ascend, and tell if ere this day,
A fairer prize was seen at sea.

Blow, but gently blow, fair wind,
From the forsaken shore,
And be as to the halcyon kind
Till we have ferried o'er,
So may'st thou still have leave to blow
And fan the way where she shall go.

From Davenant, whose "Gondibert" deserves to be better known, if it were only for the excellence of its stately preface, we copy the following. It is not a very good song, but there is a pleasant exaggeration of fancy in it, which is one of the prerogatives of knightly lovers, and we can pardon much to a man who prevented a dissolute tyrant from " lifting his spear against the muse's bower" of the blind old republican, who was even then meditating Paradise Lost.

The lark now leaves his watery nest,
And climbing, shakes his dewy wings;
He takes this window for the East,
And to implore your light he sings :

' Awake, awake, the morn will never rise
Till she can dress her beauty at your eyes.

The merchant bows unto the seaman's star,
The ploughman from the sun his season takes,
But still the lover wonders what they are,
Who look for day before his mistress wakes ;
Awake, awake! break through your veils of lawn,
Then draw your curtains and begin the dawn!'

Immediately after the old dramatists come a swarm of song-writers, of whom Herrick is perhaps the best and most unconscious. With great delicacy of sentiment, he often writes with a graceful ease of versification, and a happiness of accent unusual in his time. Very aptly did he name his poems " Hesperides," for a huge dragon of grossness and obscenity crawls loathsomely among the forest of golden apples. We extract his well-known " Night-piece " to Julia, as a good specimen of his powers. Many detached fragments of his other poems would make beautiful and complete songs by themselves.

Her eyes the glow-worm lend thee,
The shooting stars attend thee,
And the elves also,
Whose little eyes glow
Like sparks of fire, befriend thee !

No will-o'-the-wisp mislight thee,
Nor snake nor slow-worm bite thee;
 But on, on thy way,
 Not making a stay,
Since ghosts there's none to affright thee!

Let not the dark thee cumber;
What though the moon does slumber,
 The stars of the night
 Will lend thee their light
Like tapers clear without number!

Then, Julia, let me woo thee
Thus, thus to come unto me;
 And, when I shall meet
 Thy silvery feet,
My soul I'll pour unto thee!

William Habington would deserve a place
here, if it were only for the tender purity of
all his poems. They were addressed to the
woman who afterward became his wife, and are
worthy of a chaste and dignified love. His
poems are scarcely any of them good songs, and
the one we quote is more remarkable for a delicate sympathy with outward nature, which is one
of the rewards of pure love, than for melody.
It is " Upon Castara's departure."

Vows are vain. No suppliant breath
Stays the speed of swift-heeled death;

Life with her is gone, and I
Learn but a new way to die.
See, the flowers condole, and all
Wither in my funeral :
The bright lily, as if day
Parted from her, fades away;
Violets hang their heads, lose
All their beauty; that the rose
A sad part in sorrow bears,
Witness all these dewy tears,
Which as pearls or diamond like,
Swell upon her blushing cheek.
All things mourn, but oh, behold
How the withered marigold
Closeth up, now she is gone,
Judging her the setting sun.

From Carew's poems we have plucked one
little flower, fragrant with spring-time and
fanciful love. It is " The Primrose."

Ask me why I send you here
This firstling of the infant year,—
Ask me why I send to you
This primrose all bepearled with dew,—
I straight will whisper in your ears,
The sweets of love are washed with tears:
Ask me why this flower doth show
So yellow, green and sickly, too,—
Ask me why the stalk is weak
And bending, yet it doth not break,
I must tell you these discover
What doubts and fears are in a lover.

Lovelace is well known for his devoted loyalty as well as for the felicity of expression, and occasional loftiness of feeling which distinguishes his verses. The first stanza of his address to a grasshopper is wonderfully summerlike and full of airy grace.

> Oh, thou that swingest in the waving hair
> Of some well-filled oaten beard,
> Drunk every night with a delicious tear
> Dropt thee from heaven—

We copy his admired poem, "To Lucasta on going to the wars."

> Tell me not, sweet, I am unkind,
>   That from the nunnery
> Of thy chaste breast and quiet mind
>   To war and arms I fly.
>
> True, a new mistress now I chase
>   The first foe in the field,
> And with a stronger faith embrace
>   A sword, a horse, a shield.
>
> Yet this inconstancy is such
>   As you too shall adore;
> I could not love thee, dear, so much,
>   Loved I not honour more.

Cowley's "Grasshopper," founded on, rather than translated from, Anacreon, has all the spontaneous merit of an original song. We should quote it had we room. Waller, whose

fame as a poet far excels his general merit,
wrote two exquisite songs—"On a Rose," and
"On a Girdle." This last we extract. The
closing lines of the song are in the happiest vein
of extravagant sentiment.

> That which her slender waist confined,
> Shall now my joyful temples bind:
> No monarch but would give his crown,
> His arms might do what this has done.
>
> It was my heaven's extremest sphere,
> The pale which held that lovely deer:
> My joy, my grief, my hope, my love,
> Did all within this circle move!
>
> A narrow compass! and yet there
> Dwelt all that's good, and all that's fair:
> Give me but what this riband bound,
> Take all the rest the sun goes round!

Milton's songs are worthy of him. They are
all admirable, and we can only wonder how
the same spirit which revelled in the fierce in-
vective of the "Defense against Salmasius"
could have been at the same time so tenderly
sensitive. The lines which we copy can scarce
be paralleled in any language.

> Sabrina fair,
> Listen where thou art sitting
> Under the glassy, cool, translucent wave,
> In twisted braids of lilies knitting

The loose train of thine amber-dropping hair;
Listen, for dear honour's sake,
Goddess of the silver lake,
Listen and save!

The true way of judging the value of any
one of the arts is by measuring its aptness and
power to advance the refinement and sustain the
natural dignity of mankind. Men may show
rare genius in amusing or satirizing their fellow-
beings, or in raising their wonder, or in giving
them excuses for all manner of weakness by
making them believe that, although their nature
prompts them to be angels, they are truly no
better than worms,—but only to him will death
come as a timely guide to a higher and more
glorious sphere of action and duty, who has
done somewhat, however little, to reveal to its
soul its beauty, and to awaken in it an aspiration toward what only our degradation forces us
to call an ideal life. It is but a half knowledge
which sneers at *utilitarianism*, as if that word
may not have a spiritual as well as a material
significance. He is indeed a traitor to his better
nature who would persuade men that the use of
anything is proportioned to the benefit it confers
upon their animal part. If the spirit's hunger

be not satisfied, the body will not be at ease,
though it slumber in Sybaris and feast with
Apicius. It is the soul that makes men rich or
poor, and he who has given a nation a truer
conception of beauty, which is the body of
truth, as love is its spirit, has done more for its
happiness and to secure its freedom than if he
had doubled its defences or its revenue. He who
has taught a man to look kindly on a flower or
an insect, has thereby made him sensible of the
beauty of tenderness toward men, and rendered
charity and loving kindness so much the more
easy, and so much the more necessary to him.
To make life more reverend in the eyes of the
refined and educated may be a noble ambition
in the scholar or the poet, but to reveal to the
poor and ignorant and degraded those divine
arms of the eternal beauty which encircle them
lovingly by day and night, to teach them that
they also are children of one Father, and the
nearer haply to his heart for the very want and
wretchedness which half-persuaded them they
were orphan and forgotten, this, truly, is the
task of one who is greater than the poet or the
scholar, namely, a true man,—and this belongs

to the song-writer. The poet, as he wove his
simple rhymes of love, or the humble delights
of the poor, dreamed not how many toil-worn
eyes brightened and how many tyrant hearts
softened with reviving memories of childhood
and innocence. That which alone can make
men truly happy and exalted in nature is freedom ; and freedom of spirit, without which mere
bodily liberty is but vilest slavery, can only be
achieved by cultivating men's sympathy with
the beautiful. The heart that makes free only
is free, and the tyrant always is truly the bondman of his slaves. The longing of every soul
is for freedom, which it gains only by helping
other souls to theirs. The power of the song-
writer is exalted above others in this, that his
words bring solace to the lowest ranks of men,
loosing their spirits from thraldom by cherishing
to life again their numbed and deadened sympathies, and bringing them forth to expand and
purify in the unclouded, impartial sunshine of
humanity. Here, truly, is a work worthy of
angels, whose brightness is but the more clearly
visible when they are ministering in the dark
and benighted hovels of life, and whose wings

grow to a surer and more radiant strength, while they are folded to enter these humblest tenements of clay, than when they are outspread proudly for the loftiest and most exulting flight. The divinity of man is indeed wonderful and glorious in the mighty and rare soul, but how much more so is it in the humble and common one, and how far greater a thing is it to discern and reverence it there! We hear men often enough speak of seeing God in the stars and the flowers, but they will never be truly religious till they learn to behold him in each other also, where he is most easily yet most rarely discovered. But to have become blessed enough to find him in anything is a sure pledge of finding him in all; and many times, perhaps, some snatch of artless melody floating over the land, as if under the random tutelage of the breeze, may have given the hint of its high calling to many a soul which else had lain torpid and imbruted. Great principles work out their fulfilment with the slightest and least regarded tools, and destiny may chance to speak to us in the smell of a buttercup or the music of the commonest air.

ELIZABETHAN DRAMATISTS
OMITTING SHAKESPEARE

♈♈ The Plays of George Chapman

.   .   .   .   Who reads
Incessantly, and to his reading brings not
A spirit and judgment equal or superior,

*   *   *   *   *

Uncertain and unsettled still remains,
Deep versed in books and shallow in himself.

—Paradise Regained.   Book iv., 323-327

Our loftier brothers, but one in blood,
By bed and table they lord it o'er us
With looks of beauty and words of good.

—Sterling

THE appearance of an article on the old English Dramatists in a "Miscellany of Literature and Fashion," seems, at first sight, as much out of place as Thor's hammer among a set of jeweller's tools, or Roland's two-handed sword on the thigh of a volunteer captain on parade day. Yet is true poetry out of place no where, and a good word spoken for her will always find some willing and fruitful ear. For, under this thin crust of fashion and frivolity throb the undying fires of the great soul of man, which is the fountain and centre of all poesy, and which will one day burst forth, and wither like grassblades all the temples and palaces which form and convention have heaped over it. Behind the blank faces of the weak and thoughtless we see this awful and mysterious presence as we have seen one of Allston's paintings in a ballroom overlooking with its serene and steadfast eyes the butterfly throng beneath it, and seeming to gaze from these narrow battlements of time far out into the infinite promise of eternity, and see there the free, erect, and perfected soul.

It is the high and glorious vocation of poesy to make our daily life and toil more beautiful and holy by the divine ministerings of love. She is love's apostle, and the very almoner of God. She is the home of the outcast and the wealth of the needy. For her the hut becomes a palace, whose halls are guarded by the gods of Phidias and made peaceful by the maid-mothers of Raphael. She loves better the poor wanderer whose bare feet know by heart all the freezing stones of the pavement than the rich maiden for whose tender soles Brussels and Turkey are overcareful; and we doubt not but some remembered scrap of childish song has often been a truer alms than all the benevolent societies could give. The love of the beautiful and true, like the dewdrop in the heart of the crystal, remains forever clear and liquid in the inmost shrine of man's being, though all the rest be turned to stone by sorrow and degradation. The angel who has once come down into the soul, will not be driven thence by any sin or baseness. At the soul's gate sits she silently, with downcast eyes and folded hands, but, at the least

touch of nobleness, those patient orbs are up-
lifted and the whole soul is filled with their
prayerful lustre.

Over all life broods poesy, like the calm blue
sky with its motherly, rebuking face. She is
the true preacher of the word, and, in the time
of danger and trouble, when the established
shepherds have cast down their crooks and fled,
she tenderly careth for the flock. On her calm
and fearless heart rests weary freedom when all
the world have driven her from their door with
scoffs and mockings. From her white breast
flows the strong milk which nurses our patriots
and martyrs, and she robs the fire of heat, makes
the axe edgeless, and dignifies the pillory or the
gallows. She is the great reformer, and where
the love of her is strong and healthy, wicked-
ness and wrong cannot long prevail. The more
this love is refined and cultivated, the more do
men strive to make their outward lives rhythmical
and harmonious, that they may accord with that
inward harmony and rhythm by whose key the
composition of all noble and worthy deeds is
guided. It is this love which we shall endeavour

to foster and increase in our poetical extracts
and criticisms ; for it profits more to point out
one beauty than to sneer at a thousand faults.
If we can make one object in outward or inward
nature more beautiful and holy to the heart of
one of our readers, it will be reward enough. For
the more sympathies we gain or awaken for
beautiful things, by so much deeper will be our
sympathy with that which is most beautiful,—
the human soul.   Love never contracts its
circles.   They widen by as fixed and sure a law
as those round a stone cast into still waters.
The angel of love, when, full of sorrow, he followed the exiles from paradise, unwittingly
snapt off and brought away in his hand a seedpod of one of the never-fading flowers which
grew there.   Into all the dreary and desolate
places of life fell some of its blessed kernels,

> Sowing the common earth with golden seed,
> Bright as if dropt down from the galaxy.

They needed little soil to root themselves in, and
in this narrow patch of our clay they sprang
most quickly and sturdily.   Gladly they grew,
and from them all time has been sown with

whatever gives a higher hope to the soul or makes life nobler and more godlike, while, from the overarching sky of poesy, sweet dew forever falls to nourish and keep them green and fresh from the world's dust.

The old English Dramatists ! with what a glorious mingling of pride and reverence do we write these four words. Entering the enchanted realm which they " rule as their demesne," we fell like the awe-stricken Goth when his eyes drooped beneath the reverend aspects of the Roman Senate and he thought them an assembly of gods ; or more like him who, in searching the windings of a cavern, came suddenly on King Arthur and his knights seated, as of yore, about the renowned round-table. Silent and severe they sit, those men of the old, fearless time, and gaze with stern eyes upon the womanly newcomer whose back had never been galled by the weary harness, and whose soft arm had never held the lance in rest. We feel, when we come among them, that their joys and sorrows were on a more Titanic scale than those of our day. It seems as if we had never suffered

and never acted, and yet we feel a noble spur
and willingness to suffer and to act. They
show us the nobleness and strength of the soul,
and, after reading them, the men we see in the
streets seem nobler and grander, and we find
more sympathy and brotherhood in their faces.
Their works stand among those of the moderns,
like the temples and altars of the ancient inhab-
itants of this continent among the rude hovels
patched together by a race of descendants ignorant of their use and origin. Let us muse
awhile in this city of the past, and sketch
roughly some of the mighty monuments standing therein.

In the writings of the old Dramatists there is
a beauty of health and strength. Sorrow there
is,—as there is in life,—but it is a sorrow that
sympathizes with all men, and is not warped into
a gloomy and unnatural misanthropy. They
wrote before the good English word " feeling "
had whined itself into the French one " sentiment." They were too strong to need to
shelter themselves in sentimentalism, and they
thought it a worthier and more poetical ambition

to emulate the angels in love than the devils in scorn and hate. Byronism would have stood with numbed limbs and chattering teeth in the sharp, bracing mountain air which was a need to them. Yet there, amid the bare, majestic rocks, bloom tender Alpine flowers of delicatest hues and rarest fragrance, and the sturdy moss creeps everywhere with its sunny, heartfelt green.

We shall begin with George Chapman, author of the best translation of Homer, and friend of Spenser, Shakespeare, Marlow, and the other great spirits of his day. Our object is to cull out and give to our readers the most striking and beautiful passages in those of his plays which are accessible to the American critic, adding a few explanatory notices and criticisms of our own. We shall punctuate the passages selected in our own way, for we have generally found that the labours of the commentators were like the wind Cecias, whose characteristic it was, according to Aristotle, to gather clouds rather than dispel them.

Chapman is a very irregular writer. He seems like a hoodwinked eagle. Sometimes, led

by an ungovernable burst of instinctive freedom,·
he soars far up into the clear ether of song and
floats majestical with level wings, where this
world, with all its fret and turmoil, shows in the
blue distance like a silent star,—and then as suddenly he will dash down again and almost stun
himself against the noisy and dusty earth.   He
has but little dramatic power,—that Mesmerism
by which Shakespeare makes his characters
speak and act his own thoughts without letting
any of his own individuality appear in the matter,
—and his plays, taken as wholes, are not very
interesting, but they abound in grand images and
lines full of an antique and majestic favour.   In
didactic and moral passages he comes nearer to
Shakespeare than does any other of the old
Dramatists.

A mistaken opinion that the tragedies of Chapman were turgid and bombastic has prevented
the editors of old plays from reprinting them.
We think the extracts we shall give will fully
refute any such assertion.   Our first extracts
are from " Bussy D'Ambois," a tragedy.   We
first meet the hero, a brave soldier in reduced

circumstances, entering in " mean apparel." His soliloquy, which opens the play, is very fine. We wish we had room for the whole. We quote the concluding lines :

> *Man is a torch borne in the wind :* a dream
> But of a shadow, summ'd with all his substance ;—
> And, as great seamen, using all their wealth
> And skills in Neptune's deep, invisible paths,
> In tall ships richly built and ribbed with brass,
> To put a girdle round about the world,
> When they have done it (coming near their haven)
> Are fain to give a warning piece and call
> A poor stayed fisherman, that never past
> His country's sight, to waft and guide them in ;—
> So, when we wander farthest through the waves
> Of glassy glory and the gulfs of state,
> Topp'd with all titles, spreading all our reaches
> As if each private arm would sphere the earth,
> We must to virtue for our guide resort,
> Or we shall shipwreck in our safest port.

We can hardly persuade ourselves that the grand metaphor with which our extract opens did not come from Hebrew lips. The likening of virtue, also, to the fisherman that never past his country's sight is very beautiful; and we confess we are even willing to be pleased with the length and intricacy of the comparison, were it only for its reminding us so much of the golden-mouthed Jeremy Taylor.

No man ever had a larger or nobler idea of the might and grandeur of the human soul than Chapman.   He had a great deal of that exulting feeling of strength and self-help which contemporaries call conceit and posterity glorifies as the instinct and stamp of greatness.   It is a something which we find in the lives of all great men, —a recollection of wings, as it were, which enables them,

Remembering still their former height, *

to rise above these lower regions of turmoil into a clearer and serener air.   It is a feeling of trustfulness which is needful to those who cast their seed upon these waters of time that it may float down and come to fruitage in eternity, and who are glad to give up the harlot of kisses of the venial present (so bewitching to small-souledness), and find their strength and solace in the

* Marvell.

prophetic eyes of that infinite To-morrow on whose great heart they rest secure,

> Feeling through all this fleshy dress
> Bright shoots of everlastingness. *

Chapman seems nowhere so much in his element as when he makes one of his heroes burst forth into an impetuous flood of scornful independence, asserting proudly the dignity of genius over all other dignities whatever. He was like all of his great brethren (who were the worthy forerunners of the glorious band who set forever the divine right of all temporal power beneath the feet of that diviner right of the eternal soul,) fearless and independent. Indeed, there is too much scorn and pride in him to consist with the highest genius. His independent bearing amounts often to a swagger, and is truly seldom confined within the bounds of conventional propriety. Doubtless he was of opinion that "it is better to lap one's pottage like a dog than to eat it mannerly with a spoon of the devil's giving." †
And if perhaps he sometimes went about labour-

---

* Vaughan.
† Fuller's Profane State.

iously to lap it like a dog when there was no great need,—as we have known those who foolishly thought that a certain rudeness and ungraciousness of bearing was most befitting a radical,—yet we should be ready to allow a great deal to a mistaken love of principle, when the principle is a good one, recollecting that the flanks of our own hobbies are bloody with our too fiery spurring, and that enthusiasm is the most forgiveable of faults.

We have said that Chapman had but little dramatic power. His plays seem rather to be soliloquies spoken by himself from behind the masks of the different characters, than dramas. Yet he has a great deal of knowledge of character, and shrewd remarks and little touches of nature are of frequent occurrence in his plays. We copy an instance of the latter. Tamyra, the mistress of D'Ambois, after a speech of his, says, fearful lest calling him by name might betray her,

Methinks *the man* hath answered for us well.

The brother of the King turns to her and asks,

The man ? why, madam, d' ye not know his name ?

She answers in these noble words,

> *Man is a name of honour for a king.*
> *Additions take away from each chief thing.*

Mark the skill with which she covers her re-
treat, not allowing that she knows D'Ambois,
and yet satisfying her love by construing the
epithet she had applied to him into so fine a
tribute of praise as would be content with no
place lower than the highest.

> .   .   .   I watch'd how fearfully
> And yet how suddenly he cured his lies ;
> The right wit of a woman. *

We will now go on to make some extracts
from the rest of this play and others, without
following the plot or any other order than what
fancy may dictate. Read the following as examples of his exalted ideas of greatness and of
the noble vigour and stateliness which fill his
verse as he expresses them :

> ɩ   .   His words and looks
> Are like the flashes and the bolts of Jove ;
> *His deeds inimitable, like the sea*
> *That shuts still as it opes, and leaves no tracks*
> *Nor prints of precedent for mean men's facts.*

---

* Beaumont and Fletcher's Love's Pilgrimage, A. ii, S. 2

In the next extract we must call the reader's notice to the great beauty of the third line, which we cannot read without a feeling of emotion like that of the stars,—so serene and steadfast that it scarce " knows itself from rest,"— yet mingled with a wavy feeling of the sea:

> His great heart will not down : 't is like the sea,
> That, partly by his own internal heat,
> Partly the stars' daily and nightly motion,
> Their heat and light,   .   .   .
>   .   .   .   but chiefly by the moon,
> Bristled with surges, never will be won,
> (No, not when the hearts of all those powers are burst,)
> To make retreat into his settled home
> *Till he be crowned with his own quiet foam.*

How exquisite, too, is the last line of this fine comparison ! The passage seems to swell on and on, as a wave upon the beach, till it breaks into the quiet foam of the last line, and slides gently to its rippling close.

> Give me a spirit that on Life's rough sea
> Loves to have his sails filled with a lusty wind
> Even till his sailyards tremble, his masts crack,
> And his rapt ship run on her side so low
> That she drinks water and her keel plows air :
> *There is no danger to a man who knows*

What Life and Death are : there 's not any law
Exceeds his knowledge ; neither is it lawful
That he should stoop to any other law :
He goes before them and commands them all
Who to himself is a law rational.

The first few lines of this extract show well the
natural impetuosity of feeling which so much
distinguished Chapman's character, as we gather
it from his works ; and the last six exhibit the philosophic gravity and wisdom to which he had
tempered it by habits of reflection and the life of
a scholar. He was one of those incongruities
which we often meet,—a man calm and lofty in
his theory, but vehement and fiery to excess in
action, whose stillness seems, like the sleep of
the top, to arise from intensity of motion.

The same spirit shows itself in all Chapman's
characters. Even their humility is but a kind
of pride,—as we see often vanity and dandyism
showing through a Quaker coat. In Byron's
Conspiracy, the Hero says,

To fear a violent-good abuseth goodness :
'T is immortality to die aspiring,
As if a man were taken quick to heaven ;
What will not bold perfection let it burst.
.   .   .   To have stuff and form

And to lie idle, fearful and unused,
Nor form nor stuff shows.   Happy Semele
That died comprest with glory.   *Happiness*
Denies comparison of less or more,
And, not at most, is nothing.   Like the shaft
Shot at the sun by angry Hercules
And into shivers by the thunder broken,
Will I be if I burst : and in my heart
This shall be written,—that it was high and right.

Chapman's pride has, at least, all the grandeur
in it that pride can ever have.   What a glorious
comparison is that of the shaft of Hercules !
Even his devils are still Chapman.   The Evil
Spirit says to Bussy,

Why calledst thou me to this accursed light
For these light purposes ?   I am Emperor
Of *that inscrutable darkness where are hid*
All deepest truths and secrets never seen,
All which I know, and command legions
Of knowing spirits that can do more than these.
Any of this my guard that circle me
In these blue fires, *from out of whose dim fumes*
Vast murmurs use to break, and from their sounds
Articular voices, can do ten parts more
Than open such slight truths as you require.

We know of nothing in " Marlow's mighty
line " grander than this.   Ford's description of
Hell (if we recollect it rightly) seems too much

like a bill of particulars, and has a kind of ditto-ditto air which falls immeasurably below the mysterious and half-hidden grandeur of these lines.

There is one more passage which we must copy, doing honour to Chapman as a lover of freedom and as a man, and part of which seems a prophecy of what was done by those who forty years after wrote the second Magna Charta in the blood of King Charles:

> A man . . that only would uphold
> Man in his native nobleness, from whose fall
> All our dissentions rise ; that in himself
> (Without *the outward patches of our frailty,*
> *Riches and honour,*) knows he comprehends
> Worth with the greatest : kings had never borne
> Such boundless empire over other men,
> Had all maintained the spirit and state of D'Ambois ;
> *Nor had the full, impartial hand of Nature,*
> *That all things gave in her original*
> *Without these definite terms of mine and thine,*
> *Been turned unjustly to the hand of Fortune,*
> *Had all preserved her in her prime like D'Ambois ;*
> *No envy, no disjunction had dissolved*
> *Or plucked one stick out of the golden faggot*
> *In which the world of Saturn bound our lives,*
> *Had all been held together with the nerves,*
> *The genius, and the ingenius soul of D'Ambois.*

By this time we have gained a very good in-sight into the leading features of Chapman's character. Now let us see how such a man would die :

>   .   .   .   Let me alone in peace ;
> Leave my soul to me, whom it most concerns,
> You have no charge of it ; *I feel her free,*
> *How she doth rouse, and, like a falcon, stretch*
> *Her silver wings, as threatening death with death,*
> *At whom I joyfully will cast her off.*

This is very grand, but there is too much of defiance in it ; it is not so grand as the death of one would be who had learned that

> Patience and gentleness are power, *

and to whom death could never come as an enemy to cut off life too shortly, but rather as God's messenger to crown the elected one and clothe him in white raiment wherein he should shine forever. " The great, good man " has

>   .   .   .   Three sure friends,
> Himself, his Maker, and *the Angel Death.* †

Let us read the death-scene of another of his heroes :

---

* Leigh Hunt.
† Coleridge.

I'll not complain to earth yet, but to heaven,
And (like a man) look upwards even in death :
And if Vespasian thought in majesty
An emperor might die standing, why not I ?
                    (*One offers to help him.*)
Nay, without help, in which I will exceed him,
For he died splinted with his chamber-grooms.
Prop me, true sword, as thou hast ever done ;
The equal thought I bear of Life and Death
Shall let me faint on no side : I am up
Here like a Roman statue, I will stand
Till Death doth make me marble.

This is great, but it is the greatness of a
heathen ; of one, too, who, no doubt, would
make an aristocracy in death, and prefer the
respectability of the axe to the degradation of
the cross or gallows ; for there are those who
seem willing to carry only the vanities of life
out of it, and would have a blazon of arms from
the heralds' college buried with them,—as the
Norsemen did arms of a more serviceable kind,
for their use in the next world,—as a certificate
of admission to the " higher circles."

But let us hear the last :

Oh, frail condition of strength, valour, virtue
In me (like warning fire upon the top
Of some steep beacon on a steeper hill,)

Made to express it !   Like a falling star
Silently glanced, that, like a thunderbolt,
Looked to have struck and shook the firmament !

We see that the " equal thought " which, in the
moment of inspiring exultation at the idea of
dying more nobly than an emperor, he imagined
that he bore of life and death, breaks under him
as earth crumbles away from beneath his feet.
To all men the moment of death is one of inspiration ;—a feeling of grandeur and sublimity
must swell in the heart of the meanest man, as
earth swims away from under and leaves him,
alone, on his new-born wings, in the great, void
infinite.   There are men whose chrysalides
seem to have burst and their angel wings to
have expanded in this life, so that they can at
any time rise to that clear-aired point of vantage,
—men whose bodies seem only given to make
their souls visible and capable of action while
they are ministers of God's providence to their
brothers.   But Chapman seems not to have
been one of these

.   .   World's high priests, who do present
The sacrifice for all. *

* Herbert.

He was one of those impulsive natures the fruit
of whose age is not answerable to the abundant
blossoming of their youth,—who expend in a
few dazzling flashes that which if equally circu-
lated and dispensed might have been a part of
the world's healthful atmosphere. Such men
must feel in dying that their lives are incom-
plete, and must taste the overwhelming bitterness of knowing what they had so carefully
concealed from themselves, that " might have
been " can bear but a moment's semblance of
" was," from which it differs as much as the
silent glancing of a meteor from the perfect cir-
cling and fulfilment of a majestic star. He
knew not how

> To glorify his greatness with humility, *

a plant, which, humble and despised of men,
grows to be the trunk of lofty and secure self-
sustainment in the next world, while pride cannot take root in any soil less gross than that of
this.

Let us see how Chapman could describe outward nature. His natural scenery was mostly

* Ford.

that of the soul, and that, as we have seen,
rather of an Alpine character. There is none
of that breezy, summer-like feeling in him
which pervaded the verses of some of the lyric
poets a short time after, and which has come
near to perfection in many descriptive poems of
our day,

> Annihilating all that 's made
> To a green thought in a green shade, *

and seeming to be translations from the grasshopper, butterfly, locust, and bee languages into
the vernacular; yet he has some passages of
great merit in this kind. The following lines
make one feel as if he had suddenly thrown up
the window of a close and dazzling room and
looked out into the vague, foreboding eyes of
night. How silent the tread of the verse is.

> Now, all ye peaceful regents of the night,
> *Silently-gliding exhalations,*
> *Languishing winds and murmuring falls of waters,*
> *Sadness of heart and ominous secureness,*
> Enchantments, dead sleeps, all ·the friends of rest
> That ever wrought upon the life of man,
> Extend your utmost strengths, and *this charm'd hour*
> *Fix like the centre.*

---

* Marvell.

This is the perfection of descriptive poetry, painting, not the things themselves, but their effects upon the soul reflected and giving colour to them. This next is very beautiful, also:

>   .   .   .   *like a calm*
> *Before a tempest, when the silent air*
> *Lays her soft ear close to the earth to hearken*
> *For that she fears steals on to ravish her.*

Here is another exquisite touch:

> *As* when the moon hath *comforted the night*
> *And set the world in silver of her light,*
> The planets, asterisms, and whole state of heaven,
> In beams of gold descending   .   .   .

Most of the dramatists of Chapman's time excel in drawing the characters of women. This was probably the result of the greater freedom of intercourse between men and women at that day. We have grown so delicately decent, nowadays, that we must needs apologize for Nature, and make God himself more *comme il faut*. Women, who stint not in large assemblies to show that to the eyes of strangers which the holy privacy of home is not deemed pure enough to look upon, would yet grow crimson to the ears, and stare a modest horror at one who dared to call by name that which, in the loved one, is the type of all maidenhood and sweetest retirement,—in the wife, of all chastity and whitest thoughts,—and in the mother, of all that is most tender and bounteous. On such a bosom, methinks, a rose would wilt and the snowy petals of a lily drop away in silent, sorrowful reproof. We have grown too polite for what is holiest, noblest and kindest in the social relations of life; but, alas! to lie, to blush, to conceal, to envy, to sneer, to be illiberal,—these trench not on the bounds of any modesty, human or divine. Yea, " our English, the language of men ever famous and foremost in the achievements of liberty," and " which could not easily find servile words enow to spell the dictatory presumption " of an " imprimatur," * is become so slavish and emasculate † that our

---

* Milton's Areopagitica.

† " The homely but scriptural appellation by which our fathers were wont to designate the Church of Rome, has been delicately softened down by later writers. I have seen her somewhere called the Scarlet Woman, —and Helen Maria Williams names her *the Dissolute* of Babylon."

Southey.—Note to the Poet's Pilgrimage.

glorious Spensers, Taylors, and Miltons, would
find their free natures inapt to walk in its fet-
ters,—golden, indeed, and of cunningest Parisian
workmanship, but whose galling the soul is not
nice enough to discern from that of iron. The
homely names of Man and Woman which took
shelter in the cottage and the farmhouse from
the luxury, effeminacy, and vice of the city and
the court, must now be driven thence also, and
our very dairymaids and ploughmen must be
gentlemen and ladies. Let us then, in the name
of what is most polite and refined, call our
homes papaland or mamacountry, and leave the
names of father, and mother, and wife, of man
and woman, to those who are ignorant or gross
enough to be natural. Let us forget that we ever
so far yielded to the demoralizing tendency of our
baser natures as to have been suckled at our
mothers' breasts, and repent in white kid gloves
and French boots (since sackcloth and ashes are
out of the question) the damnable heresy of our
childhood, when we thought (nay, almost believed) that truth was respectable, and that
woman had any other natural developments

than head and arms. Alas! we fear that we
are wasting quite too much on these earthly
tabernacles, (resembling too nearly those who
spend their all in a costly mansion), and that the
devil will one day make a sheriff's sale of our
souls to pay for it.

We have been led away from our subject
farther, perhaps, than was needful. If we are
misinterpreted, we shall let another and worthier
plead for us :—"If any man will snatch the
pure taper from my hand and hold it to the
devil, he will only burn his own fingers, but
shall not rob me of the reward of my care and
good intentions." *

Let us read together Chapman's description
of a noble woman :

> Noble she is by birth *made good by virtue,*
> Exceeding fair, and *her behaviour to it*
> *Is like a singular musician*
> *To a sweet instrument,* or else as doctrine
> Is to the soul that puts it into act
> And prints it full of admirable forms,
> Without which 't were an empty, idle flame ;
> Her eminent judgment to dispose these parts

---

* Jeremy Taylor. Holy Living, ch. ii. sec. iii.

Sits on her brow and holds a silver sceptre
Wherewith she keeps time to the several musics
Plac'd in the sacred consort of her beauties;
Love's complete armory is managed in her
To stir affection, and the discipline
To check and to affright it from attempting
Any attaint *might disproportion her*
Or make her graces less than circular :
Yet her even carriage is as far from coyness
As from immodesty ; in play, in dancing,
In suffering courtship, in requiting kindness,
In use of places, hours and companies,
Free as the sun and nothing more corrupted ;
As circumspect as Cynthia in her vows,
As constant as the centre to observe them ;
Ruthfull and bounteous, never fierce nor dull,
In all her courses ever at the full.

Truly, this is, as one of Chapman's contemporaries called poetry, " the verie phrase of angels." A woman like this we can love, and feel that it is herein that we are made in the image of God. Such an one makes love what it should be, venerable and reverend, not a thing to be lightly treated and put off like a glove.

For love is lord of truth and loyaltie,
Lifting himselfe out of the lowly dust
On golden plumes up to the purest skie,
Above the reach of loathly, sinful lust ;

Such is the powre of that sweet passion
That it all sordid baseness doth expell
And the refined mind doth newly fashion
Unto a fairer forme. *

Having made an extract from " our sage and serious poet Spenser, whom I dare be known to think a better teacher than Scotus or Aquinas," † we must please ourselves still farther by copying a lovely picture of his which will hang fitly beside that of Chapman :

There dwell sweet love and constant chastitie,
Unspotted faith and comely womanhood,
Regard of honour and mild modestie ;
There Vertue raignes as queene in loyall throne
And giveth lawes alone
The which the base affections doe obey,
And yeeld their services unto her will,
No thought of thing uncomely ever may
Thereto approach to tempt her mind to ill. ‡

We wish we had room to copy, in this place, Jeremy Taylor's character of the Countess of Carberry, and Tennyson's Isabel,—both of them poems in the truest and highest sense of the word. The exquisite description of a virtuous

* Spenser's " Hymne of Love."
† Milton's Areopagatica.
‡ Epithalamion.

woman in the Proverbs we need only allude to.
They are all beautiful examples and encouragements to those whose care, like that of Milton's
" virtuous young lady,"

> .   .   Is fixed, and still attends
> To fill their odorous lamps with deeds of light
> And hope that reaps not shame.

We love to present them to those of our
countrywomen who read our pages. Where
women act out their divine mission there is no
need of societies for reformation. The memory
of the eyes that bent over him in infancy and
childhood haunts the man in all his after life.
If they were clear and holy, they will cheer and
encourage him in every deed of nobleness and
shame him out of all meannesses and compro-
mises. Hear Chapman:

> Let no man value at a little price
> A virtuous woman's counsel ; her winged spirit
> Is feathered oftentimes with heavenly words,
> And, like her beauty, ravishing and pure ;
> The weaker body, still the stronger soul.
> When good endeavours do her powers apply
> Her love draws nearest man's felicity.
> Oh, what a treasure is a virtuous wife,
> Discreet and loving! not one gift on earth

Makes a man so highly bound to heaven;
She gives him double forces to endure
And to enjoy, by being one with him,
Feeling his joys and griefs with equal sense.

But a true wife both sense and soul delights,
And mixeth not her good with any ill;
Her virtues, ruling hearts, all powers command;
All store without her leaves a man but poor,
And with her poverty is exceeding store.

Of love he says :

.   .   .   Love is Nature's second son,
Causing a spring of virtues where he shines ;
And as, without the sun, the world's great eye,
All colours, beauties, both of art and nature,
Are given in vain to men, so, *without love,*
All beauties bred in women are in vain,
All virtues born in men lie buried;
For love informs us as the sun doth colours,
And, as the sun, reflecting his warm beams
Against the earth, begets all fruits and flowers,
So love, fairshining in the inward man,
Brings forth in him the honourable fruits
Of valour, wit, virtue, and haughty thoughts,
Brave resolution and divine discourse.

But we must hasten on, for we mean to give
a taste of the quality of another of these true
men before we lay down our pen.   We shall

copy a few disconnected passages which have pleased us :

BODY AND SOUL

Our bodies are but thick clouds to our souls
Through which they cannot shine when they desire.

FEARLESS SPEECH

.   .   .   Thy impartial words
Are like brave falcons, that dare truss a fowl
Much greater than themselves.

THE PASSIONS

.   .   .   Those base foes that insult on weakness,
And still fight housed behind the shield of Nature.

The following passage, describing the inexplicable awe which comes over Bussy just before a ghost appears to him, is finely conceived and expressed :

What violent heat is this ?   Methinks the fire
Of twenty lives doth on a sudden flash
Through all my faculties : the air goes high
In this closed chamber, *and the frighted earth
Trembles and shrinks beneath me.*

We have marked many other passages, but we have already wellnigh exceeded our limits. These poor chippings will give our readers some idea of the component parts of this old rocky mountain. We take leave of George Chapman in his own noble words:

Farewell, brave relicks of a complete man!
Look up and see thy spirit made a star,
.   .   . and when thou set'st
Thy radiant forehead in the firmament
Make the vast crystal crack with thy receipt ;
Spread to a world of fire, and the aged sky
Cheer with new sparks of old humanity.

The Plays
of ♥ ♥ ♥
John Webster

WE shall now say a few words about JOHN WEBSTER, a writer who will not afford us so many beautiful extracts as Chapman, but who stands far above him in most of the qualities of a Dramatic Poet. Chapman aimed at being classical, and from the columns which he had chiselled out for his never-finished Grecian temple, we can take one and set it up alone without feeling the want of the rest of the building; or we can, at least, break off acanthus-leaves of the most delicate workmanship, and which are beautiful in themselves. But we can give no idea of the irregularly-regular, vast Gothic pile which Webster heaps together, with all its quaintness, mystery, and ever-aspiring grandeur, by any single portion small enough to come within the narrow limits of our cabinet.

In Webster's day there was no Pope whose sacred toe all must kiss on pain of excommunication from the holy Catholic established church of poesy, nor had the fountain of Castaly been consecrated into a saint's shrine to which only true believers could make pilgrimage. The poets of that day followed the unerring dictates of their own hearts, acknowledging no King Eric, the turning of whose cap could make the wind of their opinion blow whither he listed. They had no creed, or if they had, they merely (like the old Norsemen) put up a cross or hung a picture of the Virgin in the temple of Odin, and, though they acknowledged the new religion, preserved all the elements of the old in their poems and language. The French Apollo, with powdered wig and gold snuff-box, had not as yet set foot in England and established the reign of hollowness and taste. The heart had not yet grown to be ungenteel, and been sent to Coventry. The poets of those days knew nothing of " established principles," — which seem, in truth, to be little better than scarecrows set up by one-half of the world for the other half to pelt with mud. They knew that to be a slave in one thing is to be a slave in all. They had no mean fears of committing themselves, nor did they reckon gain and loss before they spoke what was given them. Their motto, the true creed of genius, was,

Give me but half your hearts, you have all mine. *

Laboursome ingenuity may, no doubt, find anachronisms in their works, and prove that they are not accordant to Aristotle, for what had they to do with time and space who laid their foundation in the depth of the infinite and eternal soul ? It is mediocrity which makes laws and sets mantraps and spring guns in the free realm of song, saying thus far shalt thou go and no further. Freedom is the only law which genius knows. Its very instinct leads it to take the side of freedom, and whenever it has prostituted its beautiful nature,

> Whose birth was of the wombe of morning dew,
> And its conception of the joyous prime, †

its garment of dignity and majesty, like the mantle in the ballad, ‡ withers away from it and leaves it abashed and shelterless in the eyes of all men. It was by their eyes always that the gods who had taken the bodies of men upon them were known, and where does

---

* Marlow's Lust's Dominion.

† Faerie Queen, b. iii. c. vi. st. 3.

‡ The boy with the mantle in Percy.

meanness so soon set her bedimming stamp as there ?

Webster was one of the boldest, freest, and wildest of these bold, free men. He had great pathos, and a gloomy imagination scarce matched by any of his contemporaries. He might be called the Coleridge of the old dramatists, with a good deal of Dante in him, too. We never go by a smithy in a misty night and see the bloody glare which bursts from all its chinks and windows without thinking of him. All old superstitions (so they were gloomy enough) seem to have found a fit soil in his mind.

We could not do him justice without copying whole scenes, for which we have not space. His " Vittoria Corombona," and " Dutchess of Malfy " are two of the most powerful productions in our dramatic literature. We must give one or two instances. His manner of killing a man is terrible enough. In the first play, Brachiano, having been poisoned, is lying on his deathbed, and two of his murderers, in the disguise of Capuchins, are pretending to confess him. They desire to be left alone with the dying man (already mad with pain) and then, revealing themselves, solace his last moments after this fashion :

Gasparo. Brachiano.
Lodovico. Devil Brachiano, thou art damned.
Gasp. Perpetually.
Lod. A slave condemned and given up to the gallows
    Is thy great lord and master.
Gasp. True ; for thou
    Art given up to the devil.

Then, after enumerating his crimes, and making sure that he knew who they were and could hear them perfectly, they wind up the ceremony with strangling him by way of extreme unction.

In "The Dutchess of Malfy," Ferdinand, brother of the duchess, having put her in a dungeon for marrying against his consent, visits her in the dark, and, in order to persuade her that her husband is dead, gives her a dead man's hand with her wedding ring on it. Then a curtain is drawn and artificial figures of her husband and children lying as if dead are shown to her. Add to this that she is confined among raving maniacs, and we have a terrible dungeon scene.

In the same play, the death of the Cardinal

is horribly contrived. Ferdinand, his brother,
having gone mad, and the Cardinal fearing that,
if any of his guests should overhear his ravings,
some of his own crimes would come to light, binds
them all by a promise not to try to find the cause
of any cries they may hear in the night, and adds
that he himself may call for help to try them.
In the night he is murdered within reach of as-
sistance, his shrieks being thought by his friends
to be mere feignings.

We must now give some proofs of his pathetic
power. In " Vittoria Corombona," the two
brothers, Marcello and Flamineo, quarrel, and the
latter comes in suddenly and stabs the former before his mother Cornelia's eyes. After his death
some one says,

He's dead. Pray, leave him, lady : come, you shall.

Cornelia. Alas ! he is not dead ; he 's in a trance. Why, here 's
nobody shall get anything by his death. Let me call him again,
for God's sake !

Carlo. I would you were deceived.

Corn. O, you abuse me, you abuse me, you abuse me ! how
many have gone away thus for lack of 'tendance ! Rear up his
head ! rear up his head ! his bleeding inward will kill him !

Hort. You see he is departed.

Corn. Let me come to him ; give me him as he is ; if he be turned to earth, let me but give him but one hearty kiss, and you shall put us both into one coffin. Fetch a looking-glass, see if his breath will not stain it ; or pull some feathers from my pillow and lay them to his lips. Will you lose him for a little painstaking ?

Hort. Your kindest office is to pray for him.

Corn. Alas ! I would not pray for him yet. He may live to lay me i' the ground and pray for me, if you 'll let me come to him.

Soon after the Duke comes in and enquires about the murder. Cornelia at first reproaches her surviving son, but the mother soon overcomes her and she strives to excuse him. In answer to the Duke she says,

> Indeed, my younger boy presumed too much
> Upon his manhood, gave him bitter words,
> Drew his sword first, and so, I know not how,
> For I was out of my wits, he fell with 's head
> Just in my bosom.

Page. This is not true, madam.

Corn. I pray thee, peace.

> One arrow 's gras'd already ; it were vain
> T' lose this for that will ne'er be found again.

Flamineo, the fratricide, is one of the best drawn scoundrels that we are acquainted with. The simplicity and naturalness of the speech which Webster puts into his mouth in another scene, where he comes in and finds his crazed mother winding Marcello's corpse, are very striking. After listening to his mother's ravings for some time, he says merely,

I would I were from hence.

This is not that stillness and calm which precedes the storm, but rather one produced by the storm itself, as we read of the ocean; which in the hurricane is sometimes smooth, being unable to raise its foamy crest for the very vehemence and pressure of the trampling winds. Like this is the speech of Ferdinand, when he first sees the body of his sister murdered by his procurement:

Cover her face : mine eyes dazzle : she died young.

How much meaning is there in those nine words! Indeed, the fortitude with which Webster often resists the enticements of effect when they would lead him away from nature, distinguishes him very favourably from Chapman and many others of his fellow-dramatists. He seldom forgets that, where it is easiest for the writer to make a long and pathetic speech, the real actor would be able to speak little, if at all.

There is one other little touch of nature so exquisitely simple and pathetic that we must copy it. It is from "The Dutchess of Malfy." Just before the duchess is to be murdered, her maid is taken from her, her last words to whom are,

> I pray thee look thou givest my little boy
> Some syrop for his cold, and let the girl
> Say her prayers ere she sleep.

We now go on to give some miscellaneous extracts, regretting that we cannot give more room to Webster, who indeed would demand an entire article to do him justice. This comparison is fine:

> Condemn you me for that the Duke did love me ?
> So may you blame some fair and crystal river
> For that some melancholick distracted man
> Hath drown'd himself in 't.

And this:

> Come, come, my lord, untie your folded thoughts
> And let them dangle loose as a bride's hair.

LUST
Lust carries her sharp whip at her own girdle.

EARTH AND HEAVEN
You shall see in the country in harvest time, pigeons, though

they destroy never so much corn, the farmer dare not present the fowling-piece to them : why ? because they belong to the lord of the manor ; whilst your poor sparrows, that belong to the Lord of Heaven, they go to pot for 't.

Here is something in the darkest style of our Rembrandt,—it is a death-scene :

> *Flamineo.* O, the way 's dark and horrid ! I cannot see :
> Shall I have no company ?
> *Vittoria.* O, yes, thy sins
> Do run before thee to fetch fire from hell
> To light thee thither.

And again :

> My soul, like to a ship in a black storm,
> Is driven, I know not whither.

One more example of his knowledge of nature and pathetic tenderness. Antonio, the husband of the duchess, after her murder, of which he has not heard, is walking with a friend in the church-yard and the echo from her tomb is made into a sort of oracle. Toward the end of the scene Antonio says,

> . . My duchess is asleep now,
> And her little ones : I hope sweetly : O, Heaven !
> Shall I never see her more ?
> *Echo.* Never see her more.
> *Anton.* I mark'd not one repetition of the echo
> But that ; and, *on the sudden, a clear light*
> *Presented me a face folded in sorrow.*

How finely the dawning of this presentiment is painted!

We end with a few striking passages which we had marked:

ACTION

O, my lord, lie not idle :
The chiefest action for a man of great spirit
Is never to be out of action.   We should think
The soul was never put into the body,
Which hath so many rare and curious pieces
Of mathematical motion, to stand still.
Virtue is ever sowing of her seeds :
In the trenches for the soldier ; in the wakeful study
For the scholar ; in the furrows of the sea
For men of our profession : of all which
Arises and springs up honour.

HARDENED GUILT

Or, like the black and melancholick yew-tree,
Dost think to root thyself in dead men's graves,
And yet to prosper ? Instruction to thee
Comes like sweet showers to overhardened ground,
They wet, but pierce not deep.

CONSCIENCE

.   .   How tedious is a guilty conscience !
When I look into the fish-ponds in my garden,
Methinks I see a thing armed with a rake
That seems to strike at me.

MORTALITY

.   .   .   This shroud
Shews me how rankly we do smell of earth
When we are in all our glory.

A WELL-ORDERED MIND

.   .   .   .   One whose mind
Appears more like a ceremonious chapel
Full of sweet music, than a thronging presence.

A WOMAN TEMPTER

Thou hast led me, like a heathen sacrifice,
With music and with fatal yokes of flowers,
To my eternal ruin.

MISFORTUNES

Things being at the worst, begin to mend : the bee,
When he hath shot his sting into your hand,
May then play with your eyelid.

We must end. We shall resume the subject in some future number, and will try to do more justice to it. We had hoped to have written something better than we have. But, alas! these children of the soul, which seem so fair and lovely at their conception and birth, become but pitiful, wreckling changelings when laid in the cradle of words. In continuing this article at another day, we shall at least have the consolation of those two fine lines of Withers', which were, it is said, Charles Lamb's favourites,

If thy muse do proudly tower,
As she makes wing she gets power.

The Plays of John Ford ♥ ♥ ♥ ♥

Or, if I would delight my private hours
With music or with poem, where, so soon
As in our native language, can I find
That solace?
        —Milton. Paradise Regained

                              Men
. . . . . who shed great thoughts
As easily as an oak looseneth its golden
    leaves
In kindly largess to the soil it grew on,
  .   .   .   .   .
Whose hearts have a look southward, and
    are open
To the whole noon of nature.
                          —Festus

THE ancients were wont to say that he who saw a god must die. Perhaps this meant simply that he who has looked deepest into the vast mysteries of being, and held closest converse with the Eternal Love, is overpowered by the yearning and necessity to speak that which cannot be spoken, and which yet seems hovering in fiery words upon the tongue. The voice of the mighty universe flows through the slender reed and shatters it with the very excess of quivering melody. Certain it is that without that law of genius which compels it to utter itself as it best may, very few great words had been spoken or great deeds done. Every great man is more or less tinged with what the world calls fanaticism. The disbelief of the whole world cannot shake the faith that he is God's messenger, which upbears him like a rock. He knows that the whole power of God is behind him, as the drop of water in the little creek feels that it is moved onward by the whole weight of the rising ocean. Unsupported by any of earth's customs or conventions, he leans wholly on the Infinite. The seal of God's commissions is set within, and they have no ribbands about them to make them respectable in the eyes of the many. Most men are fearful of visitings from the other world, and, set on by those whose interest lies mainly in this, they look with distrust, and often with hate, on him who converses with spirits. All the reliance of the seer is on what is within him. His own fiery soul—for the bush wherein God veils himself must needs burn—is all that urges him on and upholds him.

Men at first always deny the messenger of God. For the cunning devil holds a glass before their eyes which turns everything upside down and makes that seemingly come from hell which has indeed just descended, warm and fragrant, from the bosom of God. But Time can never put off Eternity more than a day;— swift and strong, with a step made majestic and irresistible by an eternal law, comes the fair To-morrow, and with it that clearer perception of the beautiful which sets another star in the fair girdle of the universe. The world is at

last forced to believe the message, but it despite-
fully uses the bearer of it. In most cases man
does not recognize the messenger until the disguise of flesh falls off and the white wings of
the angel are seen gleaming in the full sunshine
of that everlasting peace back into the home of
whose fathomless bosom their flight is turned.
If they recognize him earlier, it is with an ill
grace. Knowing that hunger is the best task-
master of the body, and always using to measure spirit by the laws of matter, in which their
skill chiefly lies, they think that it must needs
be the sharpest spur for the soul also. They
hold up a morsel of bread, as boys do to their
little dogs in the street, and tell the prophet to
speak for it. They know that he has a secret
to tell them, and they think that they must
starve it out of him, as if it were a demon. It
is true enough that hunger is the best urger of
the soul, but it is the hunger, not of the body,
but of the soul, which is love. A state of rest
and quietude in the body is the most comfortable to the happiness and serenity, and so to the
inspiration of the soul. Love, which is its nature, quickens the soul of the seer,

And then, *even of itself, it high doth climb ;*
What earst was dark, becomes all eye, all sight,
Bright starre, that, to the wise, of future things gives light. *

The distracting cares and sorrows of want
are not the best nurselings of genius. It is fit
that the great soul should pass through the fiery
furnace of sorrow, that it may come out refined
and whitened, and that it may learn its own infinite deepness and strength, which sorrow alone
can teach it. But that the fierce gnawings of
that bitter flame are consistent with the calm-
ness and serenity which are needful to the highest and noblest moments of the creative power
has never yet been proved. The prophet
knows his calling from childhood up. He
knows that he has that to say which shall make
the heart of the vast universe beat with a more
joyous peacefulness and a serener motion. As
he grows to man's estate, the sense of a duty
imposed on him by nature and of a necessary
obedience to heavenly messengers which the
world neither sees nor acknowledges, becomes
stronger and stronger. He feels his divine right

* Henry More's Psychathanasia.

of kinship, but earthly eyes cannot see the
crown which the exceeding brightness of his
forehead weaves around his head in the thick
air of this earth. He speaks his message, and
the world turns its hard face upon him, saying,
"Thou art a drone in my busy hive; why dost
thou not something?" He must elbow through
the dust and crowd of the market-place, when
he should be listening to the still, small voice of
God,—he must blaspheme his high and holy nature and harden his heart to a touchstone for
gold, when it is bursting with the unutterable
agony of a heavenly errand neglected, that bitterest feeling of "one who once had wings." *
The world has at length acknowledged his sovereignty and crowned him with a crown of
thorns.

As he has sown in the spirit, in the spirit he
shall reap also. It is true that the poet will
sing in spite of poverty or any other misery,
but we do not know how much sweeter and
clearer his song would have been had it not been
for these. The infinite harmony and beauty

* Keats's Hyperion.

which he sees and hears force him to give vent
to the glorious agony which swells his breast.

> The sweetness hath his herte persed so
> He cannot stint of singing by the way. *

But it cannot be that the haggard face of an un-
complaining wife and the love-supprest moans of
darling children do not shatter the crystal silence
of the air of song.   Is a lonely and desolate life,
or a social one, which is only social so far as it
draws want and sorrow upon the heads of those
he loves best, the fittest for him whose heart is
the chosen nest of all homelike feelings and delights, who loves his kind with a love whose
depth and purity only he can know, to whom
the gentlest offices of love, friendship, and honour belong as of right, whose pillow should
be smoothed by the white hands of purest
womanhood, and in whose path little children
should scatter lilies and violets ?   Alas ! many
beside Drummond have asked bitterly,

> Why was not I born in that golden age
> When gold yet was not known ? †

We have been led to these rather desultory

---

* Chaucer.   Prioress' Tale.
† 85th Sonnet.

reflections by having our thoughts turned to
the lives of the great men whose works we are
glancing at. Marlowe, Greene, Peele, and Nash,
have left behind them records of their struggles
with actual starvation rather than of their genius.
Those of the old dramatists who have established their fame most firmly, and whose writings do them most justice, are those whose
situation in life was easy and comfortable. We
cannot refrain from copying here a document,
touching and mournful in the extreme, inasmuch
as it shows us the haggard face behind the majestic mask of Tragedy, and turns the stately
march of the buskin into the crouching limp of
the beggar. Moreover, the name of Philip Massinger,—one of those whom we shall consider
in this article,—is attached to it. Massinger
soon found the truth of those lines written by
one almost his contemporary, and whose tearful
portrait of a dependent situation is familiar to all:

> That single Truth and simple Honestie
> Doe wander up and down despysed of all. *

He lived in want, and the only record of his
burial are these sad words :—" March 20, 1639–

---

* Spenser.   Colin Clout's come Home again.

40, buried Philip Massinger—*a stranger.*" The
document we alluded to reads as follows:

To our most loving friend, Mr. Philip Hinchlow, Esquire,
These :

Mr. HINCHLOW,—You understand our unfortunate extremi-
tie, and I doe not thinke you so void of christianitie but that you
would throw so much money into the Thames as wee request now
of you rather than endanger so many innocent lives. You know
there is x*l* more at least to be received of you for the play. We
desire you to lend us v*l* of that ; which shall be allowed to you,
without which we cannot be bayled, nor I play any more till this
be despatch'd. It will lose you xx*l* ere the end of the next weeke,
besides the hinderance of the next new play. Pray, sir, consider
our cases with humanity, and now give us cause to acknowledge
you our true friend in time of neede. We have entreated Mr.
Davison to deliver this note as well to witness your love as our
promises, and alwayes acknowledgemen to be ever,

Your most thankfull and loving friend,

NAT. FIELD.

The money shall be abated out of the money remayns for the
play of Mr. Fletcher and ours.   ROB. DABORNE.

I have ever found you a true loving friend to mee, and in soe
small a suite, it beeinge honest, I hope you will not fail us.

PHILIP MASSINGER.

> O, what avails it of immortall seed
> To beene ybred and never borne to die ;
> Farre better I it deeme to die with speed,
> Than waste in woe and wailefull miserie ?*

But let us leave so painful a theme.

---

* Faerie Queene, B. iii. ch. iv. S. 38.

We shall begin this article with extracts from the plays of John Ford. His powers have, we think, been rated too highly. That he has a great deal of tragic *excitability and enthusiasm*, and a good knowledge of stage effect, we readily admit. But these are the predominant qualities of his nature; whereas in the strong mind they are always subservient. The great dramatist uses them as means, the weaker one as ends, and is content when he has wrought himself up to a " fine madness," which is rarely consistent with sustained energy. Ford does not merit the exalted praise, which, if we remember, Lamb bestows upon him, and which other less judicious critics have repeated. The gentle lovingness of Lamb's nature fitted him for a good critic; but there was a knotty quirk in his grain, which seemed, indeed, when polished by refined study, little less than a beauty, but which led him to the worship of strange gods, and that with a more scrupulous punctuality, since the mass were of a different persuasion. No field is so small or so barren but there will be grazing enough to keep a hobby in very good case.

Lamb's love was of too wide-spreading a kind to be confined to the narrow trellises which satisfy a common nature. It stretched out its tendrils and twined around everything within its reach, clipping with its tender and delicate green alike the fair tree and the unsightly stump. Everything that he loved was for the time his ideal of loveliness. Even tobacco, when he was taking leave of it, became the very crown of perfumes, "the only manly smell," and he esteemed

> Roses and violets but toys
> For the smaller sort of boys,
> Or for greener damsels meant.

John Ford, though he cannot rank with the first order of minds, is yet one of that glorious band who so illustrated and dignified our English tongue at the beginning of the seventeenth century. Set beside almost any of our modern dramatists he has certainly somewhat of the Titan about him; and, though he has not that "large utterance" which belongs to Shakespeare and perhaps one or two others of his contemporaries, he sometimes rises into a fiery earnestness

which falls little short of sublimity, and proves
that he has in him, as was said of Marlowe,

> . . . those brave, *sublunary things*
> That our first poets had. *

It is this earnestness and simplicity which so
much elevate the writers of that age above
nearly succeeding ones. They laid the deep-
set bases of their works on the eternal rock of
Nature, not idly writing their names on the
shifting and unstable sand of a taste or a prejudice to be washed out by the next wave or over-
drifted by the first stronger breeze. Pegasus is
a very unsafe hobbyhorse. The poet whose
pen is governed by a theory, will only be read
so long as that theory is not driven out by another. Creeds, we readily admit, are often of
good service to the cause of truth. They may
consecrate the will and energy of a strong mind
on one point and so lead to the discovery of
those truths which intersect that point in their
revolutions, as the wells of the old astronomers,
by shutting out all light from around, enabled
them to see the stars. But the credit should be

---

* Drayton.

given rather to concentration and resolution than to creeds. Resolution is the youngest and dearest daughter of Destiny, and can gain of her mother any favour she chooses to ask, almost even in very wantonness. The great spirits of that day were of no "school." The door to the temple of any creed would not admit men of their godlike stature without stooping, and that they could not do. They scorned these effeminate conventionalities of fashion which soon after decked our ruddy English muse in the last Paris modes, powdered her fair golden hair, and so pinched her robust waist that she has scarce borne a healthy child since. Poesy with them was not an art which could be attained by any one who could detect the jingle of two words and count ten on his fingers. They esteemed Poesy as the most homelike and gentle of spirits, and would not suffer her to go abroad that she might bring home licentiousness veiled under a greater precision of manner at the expense of all freedom and grace. They knew that all the forms of poesy are changeable as those of a cloud. They fall away like the petals of a flower, but they leave the plain, sober seedpod which most men pass by heedlessly, but which is the source of all poesy, namely, the soul. Only that part of a form which is founded in nature can survive. The worth of the statue of Memnon as an oracle died with the wise priest who spoke through it; but, after three thousand years, it is still musical under the golden fingers of the sunrise.

It was not from ignorance of rules that the old dramatists committed anachronisms, made islands of countries set in the heart of continents, and put English oaths into the mouths of Roman mobs; they broke through them, for such cobwebs were not spun to catch eagles in. They laid their scene in the unchangeable heart of man, and so

Made one little room an everywhere. *

They mostly scorned to bow the knee to that popular idol which a voice in the depth of their hearts made them spurn. They knew full well that whoso strives to keep an act of fealty to slavery secret, does most wofully deceive his

---

*Donne. The Good Morrow.

better reason. It is as public and open as the prostration of King Ottocar. The homage that a man does in his secret soul is visible to all time. The galling mark of the fetter will never out. Men read it in every line he writes, hear it in every word he speaks, and see it in every look he looks. If he be no longer the slave of a cowardly deference to the opinions of the many, because they are so; he is still the bondman of Memory, who can make him cringe at her bidding. It may be thought that the writers of that day had no daws to peck at them. But hear what Harrington says, in an " Apologie for Poesie," * printed in 1591 :

> We live in such a time in which nothing can escape the envious tooth and backbiting tongue of an impure mouth, and wherein everie blinde corner hath a squinteyed Zoilus that can looke arighte on no man's doings.

Of all the dramatic poets of that day Shakespeare stooped the least.

But enthusiasm has led us astray. We return to Ford. His dramatic power consists chiefly in the choice of his plots. His charac-

---

* Reprinted with Puttenham's Art of English Poesy, and other valuable tracts.

ters, as is often the case with those of retired
students, are rather certain turns of mind, or
often eccentricities, put into a body, than real
men and women. His plots raise him and
carry him along with them whither they please,
and it is generally at their culminating points
alone that he shows much strength. Indeed,
we know not if this should not rather be called
weakness. He puts his characters into situa-
tions where the heart that has a drop of hot
blood in it finds it easier to be strong than weak.
His heroes show that fitful strength which
springs from an intense excitement, rather than
from a true, healthy, muscular action. Their
strength does not rise with the difficulty or danger they are in, and, looking down on it, assert
calmly the unconquerable sovereignty of the
soul, even after the body is overcome, but, in an
exulting gush of glorious despair, they spring
forward to grapple with death and fate. In a
truly noble bravery of soul the interest grows
from its immortality; here it is the fruit of
mortality. In the one case we exult to see the
infinite overshadow and dwarf the finite, in the

other we cannot restrain a certain romantic admiration at seeing the weak clay so gallantly defy that overwhelming power which it well knows must crush it. High genius may be fiery and impetuous, but it never swaggers or wears the vulgar air of the bully. It does not defy death and futurity, for a doubt of its kingship over them never overflushed the majestic havir of its serene countenance.

Shakespeare's characters modify his plots as much as his plots modify his characters. As in life, there is a perpetual seesaw of character and circumstance, now one uppermost, now the other. Nature is never afraid to reason in a circle. The actors in his dramas are only overcome by so much as they fall below their ideal, and are wanting in some attribute of true manhood. Wherever we go with him the absence of nobleness always suggests its presence. We feel in his supinest characters that

> Man is his own star, and the soul that can
> Render an honest and a perfect man
> *Commands* all light, all influence, all fate. *

---

* Fletcher. From a poem appended to The Honest Man's Fortune.

But Ford's heroes are strong only in their imper-
fection, and it is to this that what admiration we
give them is paid.   They interest us so far only
as their impetuousness can make us forget our
quiet, calm ideal.   This is the very stamp of
weakness.   We should be surprised if we saw
them show any natural greatness.   What we
call greatness and nobleness is in fact only
healthiness.   To those only who are unnatural
themselves does it seem wonderful.   To the
natural man it is as customary as the motion of
his lungs or the beating of his heart, and as
necessary.   Praise always surprises and hum-   /
bles genius.   The shadow of earth comes then
between it and its starry ideal with a cold and
dark eclipse.   In Ford's characters the sublimity is that of a defiant despair.   The man of
genius may fail, but it is never thus.   In him
the spirit often overbalances the body and sets
its ideal too far beyond the actual.   Unable to
reach it, he seems to do less than one of less
genius, for the performance, of anything lower
than what he has marked out for himself has a
feeling to him almost of degradation.   His

wings may be too weak to bear him to that infinite height, but, if he fall, he is an angel still,
and he falls not so low as the proudest pitch of
talent. His failures are more successful than
their successes. It is only little wits that are
allied to madness. " It is the ill success of our
longings that with Xerxes makes us to whip the
sea and send a cartel of defiance to Mount
Athos." * But high genius has that in it which
makes that its longings cannot be unsuccessful.

Its utmost imperfectness has always some
touch of the perfect in it.

The slavery of the character to incident in
the plays of Ford has sometimes reminded us of
the story of the travellers who lost their
way in the mummy-pits, and who were all forced
to pass through the same narrow orifice, which
readily admitted the slender ones, but through
which the stout were obliged to squeeze and
struggle with a desperate forgetfulness of bulk.
It may be foolish for a philosopher, but it is
wise for a dramatist to follow the example of
nature, who always makes large holes for her
large cats and small holes for her small ones.

* Daniel's Defense of Rime.

Ford, perhaps, more than any of his contemporaries deserves the name of *sentimental*. He has not the stately gravity nor antique majesty of Chapman, nor the wild imagination or even the tenderness of Webster; but he has more sentiment than either. The names of his plays show the bend of his mind. "Love's Sacrifice," "The Lover's Melancholy," and "The Broken Heart," are the names of three of the best; and there is another in which the doctrine of the elective affinities is laid down. *   Ford does not furnish many isolated passages which are complete in themselves, a quality remarkable in many of the old dramatists, of whom only Shakespeare united perfectness of parts with adaptation and harmony of the whole. A play of Shakespeare's seems like one of those basaltic

---

* Ford's personal appearance seems to have been answerable to what we have surmised of his character. A contemporary writer says of him very graphically,

> Deep in a dump John Ford *was alone got,*
> *With folded arms and melancholy hat,*

two lines which bring up the central figure in the frontispiece to the old editions of Burton's Anatomy of Melancholy very vividly before our eyes.

palaces whose roof is supported by innumerable pillars, each formed of many crystals perfect in themselves. As a fair way of judging Ford, we shall give a sketch of the plot of the most famous of his plays with occasional extracts.

The plot of " The Broken Heart " is simply this. Ithocles, the favourite of Amyclas King of Laconia, instigated by an ancient feud, has forced his sister Penthea who was the betrothed wife of Orgilus to marry Bassanes. Orgilus, full of an intention to revenge himself at the first chance, pretends a reconcilement with Ithocles, who meanwhile has repented of the wrong he had done, and moreover loves and is beloved by Calantha the King's daughter. Penthea dies mad. Orgilus murders Ithocles on the eve of his marriage with Calantha, who dies of a broken heart, after making Nearchus, her former suitor, her successor to the throne.

The following has great purity and beauty, and withal much sentimentalism in it. Orgilus has, in the disguise of a scholar (a disguise as common now as then), gained speech of Penthea. We copy only the last part of the scene :

Penthea. How, Orgilus, by promise I was thine,
The heavens do witness ; they can witness, too,
A rape done on my truth : how I do love thee
Yet, Orgilus, and yet, must best appear
In tendering thy freedom ; for I find
The constant preservation of thy merit,
By thy not daring to attempt my fame
With injury of any loose conceit
Which might give deeper wounds to discontent.
Continue this fair race ; then, though I cannot
Add to thy comfort, yet I shall more often
Remember from what fortune I am fallen,
And pity mine own ruin.   Live, live happy,
Happy in thy next choice, that thou may'st people
This barren age with virtues in thine issue !
And oh, when thou art married, think on me
With mercy, not contempt ; I hope thy wife,
Hearing my story, will not scorn my fall.—
Now let us part.

This is touching, though there is a little too much
of the " patient Grizzle " in it to comport with
the higher graces of the womanly character.
But to return.

Orgilus.   Part ! yet advise thee better :
Penthea is the wife to Orgilus,
And ever shall be.
    Pen.   Never shall, nor will.
    Org.   How !
    Pen.   Hear me : in a word I'll tell thee why.
The virgin dowry which my birth bestowed

Is ravished by another ; my true love
Abhors to think that Orgilus deserved
No better favour than a second bed.

 Org. I must not take this reason.

 Pen. To confirm it,
Should I outlive my bondage, let me meet
Another worse than this and less desired,
If, of all men alive, thou should'st but touch
My lip or hand again !

 Org. Penthea, now
I tell you, you grow wanton in mv sufferance ;
Come, sweet, thou art mine.

 Pen. Uncivil sir, forbear,
Or I can turn affection into vengeance :
Your reputation, if you value any,
Lies bleeding at my feet. Unworthy man,
If ever henceforth thou appear in language,
Message, or letter, to betray my frailty,
I'll call thy former protestations lust,
And curse my stars for forfeit of my judgment.
Go thou, fit only for disguise and walks
To hide thy shame ; this once I spare thy life.
I laugh at mine own confidence ; my sorrows
By thee are made inferior to my own fortunes :
If ever thou did'st harbour worthy love,
Dare not to answer. My good genius guide me
That I may never see thee more ! Go from me !

 Org. I 'll tear my veil of politic French off,
And stand up like a man resolved to do :—
Action, not words, shall show me. Oh, Penthea !

          [*Exit*

> *Pen.* He sighed my name, sure, as he parted from me ;
> I fear I was too rough.   Alas ! poor gentleman,
> He look'd not like the ruins of his youth,
> But like the ruins of those ruins.   Honour,
> How much we fight with weakness to preserve thee !

To our mind, Penthea's last speech is the best part of the scene.   She shows, in the former part, a seemingly Roman virtue, but there seems to be in it a savour of prudery and a suspicion of its own strength, which true, courageous honour and chastity would be the last to entertain.

Now let us turn to the catastrophe of the plot.   Calantha, after settling the succession to the kingdom, turns to the body of Ithocles.

> *Cal.*   Forgive me : now I turn to thee, thou shadow
> Of my contracted lord !   Bear witness all
> I put my mother's wedding-ring upon
> His finger ; 't was my father's last bequest.
> Thus I new-marry him, whose wife I am :
> Death shall not separate us.   Oh, my lords,
> I but deceived your eyes with antick gesture,
> When one news straight came huddling on another,
> Of death ! and death ! and death ! still I danced forward ;
> But it struck home, and here, and in an instant.
> But such mere women, who, with shrieks and out-cries,
> Can vow a present end to all their sorrows,
> Yet live to court new pleasures and outlive them :

They are the silent griefs which cut the heart-strings ;
Let me die smiling.
One kiss on these cold lips, my last ! [*kisses Itbocles*]
  crack—crack—
Argo now's Sparta's king. Command the voices
Which wait at the altar, now to sing the song
I fitted for my end.

Lamb speaks of this death-scene as " carrying us
back to Calvary and the Cross" (or uses words
to that effect), but this, it seems to us, is attrib-
uting too much importance to the mere physical
fact of death.   What one dies for, and not his
dying, glorifies him.   The comparison is an
irreverent one, as that must needs be which
matches a selfish with an universal love.
Love's nobility is shown in this,—that it
strengthens us to make sacrifices for others, and
not for the object of our love alone.   Our love
for one is only so made preëminent, that it
may show us the beauty and holiness of that
love whose arms are wide enough for all.   It is
easy enough to die for one we love so fiercely,
but it is a harder and a nobler martyrdom to live
for others.   Then love is perfected when it can
bear to outlast the body which was only its outward expression and a prop for its infant steps,

and can feel its union with the beloved spirit in a mild serenity and in an inward prompting to thousand little acts of everyday brotherhood. The love of one is a means not an end.

Another objection which we should feel inclined to make to this scene is that the breaking of Calantha's heart seems too palpable and physical an event. It is too much like the mere bursting of a blood-vessel, which is by no means so poetically tragic. It is like the verse of the old ballad:

> She 's turned her back unto the wall,
> And her face unto the rock ;
> *And there, before the mither's eyes,*
> *Her very heart it broke.* *

In the ballad, however, there is more propriety. The heroine's heart breaks suddenly under a sudden blow; but Calantha, as it were, saves up her heart-break until it can come in with more effect at the end of the tragedy.

Ford sometimes reminds us of the picturesque luxuriance of Fletcher. The following exquisite passage is very like Fletcher, and is a

---

* Prince Robert.   In Scott's Minstrelsy.

good specimen of Ford's lighter powers. When
we read it, we almost wish that he had written
masques or pastorals rather than plays. It is
from " The Lover's Melancholy " :

> .   .   .   One morning early
> This accident encountered me : I heard
> The sweetest and most ravishing contention
> That art and nature ever were at strife in.
> A sound of music touched mine ears, or rather
> Indeed, entranced my soul : as I stole nearer,
> Invited by the melody, I saw
> This youth, this fair-faced youth, upon his lute,
> With strains of strange variety and harmony,
> Proclaiming, as it seemed, so bold a challenge
> To the clear choristers of the woods, the birds,
> That, as they flocked about him, all stood silent,
> Wond'ring at what they heard : I wondered too.
> .   .   .   A nightingale,
> Nature's best-skilled musician, undertakes
> The challenge, and, for every several strain
> The well-shaped youth could touch, she sang her own ;
> He could not run division with more art
> Upon his quaking instrument, than she,
> The nightingale, did with her various notes
> Reply to ; for a voice and for a sound,
> Amethus, 't is much easier to believe
> That such they were, than hope to hear again.
> Some time thus spent, the young man grew at last
> Into a petty anger that a bird,

Whom art had never taught cliffs, moods, and notes,
Should vie with him for mastery, whose study
Had busied many hours to perfect practice :
To end the controversy, in a rapture,
Upon his instrument he plays so swiftly,
So many voluntaries and so quick,
That there was curiosity and cunning,
Concord and discord, lines of differing method
Meeting in one full centre of delight.
    .   .   The bird, ordained to be
Music's first martyr, strove to imitate
These several sounds ; which, when her warbling throat
Failed in, for grief, down dropt she on his lute
And brake her heart !

Now let us gather up a few of the most striking lines in his plays, and then hasten to a brief
notice of Massinger, who is, probably, better
known to most readers.

FLATTERY

    .   .   .   .   A sin
Friendship was never guilty of ; for flattery
Is monstrous in a true friend.

The metre of this next passage is very fine.
There is a sadness and weariness in the flow of
the verse which sinks gradually into the quiet of
the exquisitely modulated last line :

END OF A WASTED LIFE

Minutes are numbered by the fall of sands,
As by an hour-glass ; the span of time
Doth waste us to our graves, and we look on it :
An age of pleasures, revelled out, comes home
At last and ends in sorrow ; but the life,
Weary of riot, numbers every sand,
Wailing in sighs, until the last drop down,
So it conclude calamity in rest.

OPINION

Busy opinion is an idle fool,
That, as a schoolrod keeps a child in awe,
Fights the inexperienced temper of the mind.

THE GREAT MAN

He, in this firmament of honour, stands
Like a star fixed ; not moved with any thunder
Of popular applause, or sudden lightning
Of self-opinion.

AN OUTSIDE VIRTUE

.   .   .   No fair colours
Can fortify a building faintly joined.

REMORSE

.   .   .   My miseries
As in a glass present me the rent face
Of an unguided youth.

HUMILITY

Let upstarts exercise unmanly roughness,
Clear spirits to the humble will be humble.

INDEPENDENCE

.   .   .   I never wore
The rags of any great man's looks, nor fed
Upon their after-meals; I never crouched
Unto the offal of an office promised
(Reward for long attendance) and then missed :
I read no difference between this huge,
This monstrous big word, lord, and gentleman,
More like the title sounds ; for aught I learn,
The latter is as noble as the first,
I am sure more ancient.

What land soe'er the world's surveyor, the sun,
Can measure in a day, I dare call mine :
All kingdoms I have right to ; I am free
Of every country ; in the four elements
I have as deep a share as an emperor ;
All beasts whom the earth bears are to serve me,
All birds to sing to me ; and can you catch me
With a tempting golden apple ?

We alluded to Ford's picture of Hell in our
first article. It has certainly some fine touches
in it, but it is only a material hell, after all.

There is a place,
List, daughter ! in a black and hollow vault,
Where day is never seen ; there shines no sun,

But flaming horror of consuming fires,
A lightless sulphur, chok'd with smoky fogs
Of an infected darkness ; in this place
Dwell many thousand thousand sundry sorts
Of never-dying deaths : there damned souls
Roar without pity ; there are gluttons fed
With toads and adders ; there is burning oil
Poured down the drunkard's throat ; the usurer
Is forced to sup whole draughts of molten gold ;
There is the murderer forever stabbed,
Yet can he never die ; there lies the wanton
On racks of burning steel, whilst, in his soul,
He feels the torment of his raging lust.

Mr. Dyce, in his edition of Webster, says
that " Mr. Lamb calls this scene between Con-
tarino and Ercole, ' the model of a well-man-
aged and gentlemanlike difference.' " * We
refer the reader who is desirous of learning how
a murder may be done in the same " well-
managed and gentlemanlike " manner, to the
" Broken Heart," Act iii, S. 4. We shall end
by gleaning a few scattered lines or expressions
from the different plays.

The sweetest freedom is an honest heart.

   .   .   .   These are petty shifts
Souls bankrupt of their royalty submit to.

---

* Works of Webster, vol. ii. p. 43.

.   .   .   Cupid has broke
His arrows here ; and, like a child unarmed,
Comes to make sport between us with no weapon
But feathers stolen from his mother's doves.

.   .   .   Far better 't is
To bless the sun than reason why it shines.

.   .   .   Let not the curse
Of old prescription rend from me the gall
Of courage.

.   .   .   Time can never
On the white table of unguilty faith
Write counterfeit dishonour.

.   .   .   There is more divinity
In beauty than in majesty [royalty.]

✠ ✠ The Plays of Philip Massinger

. . . . which contain the honour of
the dead, the fame of the living, the
glory of peace, and the best power of
our speech, and wherein so many
honourable spirits have sacrificed to
memory their dearest passions, shew-
ing by what divine influence they have
been moved, and under what stars they
lived.

—Daniel's " Defense of Rime "

Whatever those inspired souls
  Were urged to express, did shake
The aged Deep, and both the Poles;
  Their numerous thunder could awake
Dull Earth, which does with Heaven
  consent
To all they wrote, and all they meant.
—Waller

LET us now turn to MASSINGER. He seems to us the Cowper of his age. If Cowper had lived then and written plays. he would have written such as " The Virgin Martyr," and " The Fatal Dowry." There is something even in Cowper's physiognomy which reminds of Massinger. In their writings we observe the same religious feeling. But Massinger's mind was too strong to admit that sentimentalism into his religious faith which characterized Cowper's. Indeed his mind was altogether of a more majestic and vigorous cast. He seldom displays fancy or tenderness, and never the highest reaches of imagination. Ford has no humour, but Massinger has almost less than none. His attempts at it are ribaldry and buffoonery, and his lower female characters, whom he evidently esteems his forte in this kind of writing, are absolutely disgusting. From this want of humour the other wants of Massinger's mind might be readily deduced. The higher quality of genius, especially in dramatic poetry, cannot consist with an absence of it.

Without it there can be little pathos and little
grandeur of imagination. It lies next to our
strongest and deepest feelings, and, indeed
seems then to be in fullest play when the mind
is most intensely excited. Beyond the deepest
sorrow in the minds of men there is a deeper
deep of humour, and they who are naturally
saturnine will often be very merry on an occasion of peculiar sadness. But in the mind of
genius, as its sorrows are more deep, so its humour is nearer the surface; and it remains naturally at that height whereto common minds only
attain under the fiercest excitement. As Spenser, Shakespeare, and Fletcher were evidently
Milton's earliest favourites, so his grave mind
was evidently attracted by Massinger, a fact not
unnoticeable as illustrating our criticism, and
which might easily be proved by parallel passages.

The foremost characteristic of Massinger,
as we gather it from his writings, is a refined
and grave dignity, fired with a certain Sir
Philip Sydneyism of chivalrous gentlemanliness,

and highly-wrought courtesy. We use the
word gentlemanliness in its first meaning, and
not as the exponent of any particular artificial
grade in society. Massinger respected rank as
being, in most cases, the representative at least
of an ancestral virtue, but he did not from the
fineness of the coat judge of the nobility of the
heart under it, nor predicate the clearness of
the spirit upon that of the skin. If he have
not so much outward independence of manner
as some of his fellow-dramatists, yet the bitter
friendlessness of his last moments proves that,
in an age of patronage, he had not stooped to
servility, which, as it starves the soul, so also
does it take the more lavish care of the body
whose pander and bawd it is. That great and
noble heart, as it turned full of an almost over-
mastering sorrow from a neglectful world
swarmed with buzzing temporalities, to the
peaceful welcome home of eternal rest and
silence, must have been taunted and mocked by
a crowd of bitter memories. But it could yet
bid farewell with an unshrinking and lofty

majesty, being yet more a king, and over wider
realms, in its dethronement than in the fullness
of its sway, since it could not be reproached
with one act of meanness or cowardice, or with
ever having put the soul in pawn to satisfy the
pampered cravings of the body. In all his poverty and low estate he did not bate a jot of
heart or hope, for these cannot but reveal to the
truly poetic spirit the full glory of its calling,
giving it a more inward and cultured sympathy
with the common wants and sorrows of humanity. How sublime becomes for us the pent-up
garret of the artist! How does the remembrance of the mighty soul which toiled there—
of that thoughtful brow and those serene, eter-
nal-looking eyes from which the spirit of an age,
rather than of a single man seems gazing—make
the narrow walls vanish so that we feel as if we
hung in the infinite abyss of space, and the little
world were but a tiny point of sparkling light
which we cannot shut out with our hand.

Massinger had nothing of the coward in him,
and never lets his respect for rank put its time-

serving hand over the mouth of his fealty to
truth and virtue.   He felt himself to be a peer
of the realms of nature, a lord spiritual in an
establishment as eternal as Truth itself, one of
those nobles whose patent we can read in their
faces, in the tone of their voice, in the grasp of
their hand; who rule over their fellow-men by
a divine right which not even time and death
dare dispute, and who leave the outward distinc-
tions of a conventional littleness to such as can
best fashion realities out of such pretty fictions.
Often he swoops down upon some knighted
vice, some meanness skulking behind a star-
breasted coat, or some beduked infamy, and
sometimes, like an eagle in a dovecot, flutters
even the dwellers within the sacred precincts of
the court itself.   Yet, while he does not bend
cap in hand before an outward and customary
superiority, he has none of that arrogant assump-
tion of equality which is indeed the basest and
most degrading kind of aristocracy.   Freedom is
all that men can lay claim to in common, and
that is no true manhood which needs comparison

with others to set it off. Massinger, as we have said, is eminent for his gentlemanlike feeling, and the true gentleman is he who knows, and knows how to gain for himself without an exaction what is his due, rather than he who gives their dues to others.—The latter needs but an exercise of justice, and is, indeed, included in the former, which must needs be endowed with patience, gentleness, humble dignity, and all the honourable and virtuous adornments of a wise and courageous humanity.

We shall copy here a few random passages from all his plays, both to illustrate what we have said and what we have yet to say of our poet.

CHARITY

      Look on the poor
With gentle eyes ! *for in such habits often*
Angels desire an alms.

AN UNCONQUERED MIND

     He that hath stood
The roughest battery that captivity
Could ever bring to shake a constant temper,
Despised the fawnings of a future greatness
By beauty in her full perfection tendered,
That hears of death as of a quiet slumber,

And from the surplusage of his own firmness
Can spare enough of fortitude to assure
A feeble woman, *will not*, Mustapha
Be altered in his soul by any torments
We can afflict his body with.

   *   *   *   *   *

.   .   .   Conquest
Over base foes is a captivity
And not a triumph. I ne'er feared to die
More than I wished to live. When I had reached
My ends in being a duke, I wore these robes,
This crown upon my head, and to my side
This sword was girt, and witness truth that, now
'T is in another's power when I shall part
With them and life together, I 'm the same :
My veins then did not swell with pride, nor now
Shrink they for fear.

MARTYRDOM

The sight of whips, racks, gibbets, axes, fires,
Are scaffolding by which the soul climbs up
To an eternal habitation.

VOX POPULI NOT ALWAYS VOX DEI

Extraordinary virtues, when they soar
Too high a pitch for common sights to judge of,
Losing their proper splendour, are condemned
For most remarkable vices.

The following fine passage is a good specimen of Massinger's most fiery style. It has

none of that volcanic aspect which startles us
into admiring wonder in Chapman, whose rust-
ling vines and calm snow-capt head, which
seems made to slumber in the peaceful blue, are
on the sudden deluged with surging lava from
the burning heart below,—none of that lightning brilliance which blurs the eyes of our better critical judgment.   It savours rather of the
dignified indignation of Tully which never forgets that it has saved Rome, and would not jar
the studied * taste of the porticoes of the Academy.

.   .   .   To you,
Whom it does most concern, my lord, I will
Address my speech, and, with a soldier's freedom,
In my reproof, return the bitter scoff
You threw upon my poverty : you contemned
My coarser outside, and from that concluded
(As by your groom you made me understand)
I was unworthy to sit at your table
Among these tissues and embroideries,

---

* We do not mean to imply any artificiality like the foresighted
pathos of Sheridan's " My gods," or the coughs of the famous
Oliver Maillard, in the manuscript of whose sermon preached at
Bruges in 1500, the words, " Hem, hem, hem," are inserted at
certain intervals.   *See note in Du Chat's Rabelais.*

Unless I changed my habit : I have done it,
And shew myself in that which I have worn
In the heat and fervour of a bloody fight ;
And then it was in fashion, not (as now)
Ridiculous and despised.   This hath past through
A wood of spikes, and every one aimed at it,
Yet scorned to take impression of their fury :
With this, as you still see it, fresh and new
I 've charged through fire that would have singed your sables,
Black fox and ermines, and changed the proud colour
Of scarlet though of the right Tyrian die.—
But now, as if the trappings made the man,
Such only are admired as come adorned
With what 's no part of them.   This is mine own,
My richest suit, a suit I must not part from,
But not regarded now : and yet, remember
' Tis we that bring you in the means of feasts,
Banquets and revels, which when you possess,
With barbarous ingratitude you deny us
To be made sharers in the harvest which
Our sweat and industry reaped and sowed for you.
The silks you wear, we with our blood spin for you ;
This massy plate, that with the ponderous weight
Doth make your cupboards crack, we (unaffrighted
With tempests, or the long and tedious way,
Or dreadful monsters of the deep that wait
With open jaws still ready to devour us)
Fetch from the other world.   Let it not then
In after ages to your shame be spoken
That you with no relenting eyes look on

Our wants that feed your plenty ; or consume,
In prodigal and wanton gifts on drones,
The kingdom's treasure, yet detain from us
The debt that with the hazard of our lives.
We have made you stand engaged for ; or force us,
Against all civil government, in armour
To require that which with all willingness
Should be tendered ere demanded.

DEATH

.   .   How the innocent
As in a gentle slumber pass away !
But to cut off the knotty thread of life
In guilty men, must force stern Atropos
To use her sharp knife often.

DOUBT

.   .   *To doubt*
Is worse than to have lost.

.   .   .   .

.   .   Where true honour lives,
Doubt hath no being.

FREEDOM

.   .   I have ever loved
An equal freedom, and proclaimed all such
As would usurp on others' liberties
Rebels to nature, to whose bounteous blessings
All men lay claim as true legitimate sons.

REVERENCE IN LOVE

Leostbenes.   Honest simplicity and truth were all
The agents I employed, and when I came

To see you, it was with that reverence
As I beheld the altars of the gods ;
And love that came along with me, was taught
To leave his arrows and his torch behind
Quenched in my fear to give offence.
    Cleora.   And 't was
That modesty that took me *and preserves me*
Like a fresh rose in mine own natural sweetness,
Which, sullied by the touch of impure hands,
Loses both scent and beauty.

DREAD

  .   .   What a bridge
Of glass I walk upon, over a river
Of certain ruin, mine own weighty fears
Cracking what should support me !

SUICIDE

  .   .   .   He
That kills himself to avoid misery fears it,
And, at the best, shows but a bastard valour.
This life 's a fort committed to my trust,
Which I must not yield up till it be forced,
Nor will I : he 's not valiant that dares die,
But he that boldly bears calamity.

PROCRASTINATION

The resolution that grows cold to-day,
Will freeze to-morrow.

But, after all, such few gleanings as we can
make in the way of extracts, can give us but a
limited idea of the quality of the field. The

general impression gathered from the man's whole works will be nearer the truth. It is the more likely to be so because in Massinger's plays the whole power of the man is plainly put forth. We do not feel in reading him, that he was

> A budding star, that might have grown
> Into a sun when it had blown. *

There is nothing rugged or precipitous in his genius, no peaks that lose themselves in the clouds,—all is smooth table land, with scarce an unevenness of surface. We never could say which of his plays was our favourite. This sustained vigour shows strength and unwearied-ness of mind rather than high poetic genius. Genius seems to want steadfastness, not by sinking below its proper pitch, but from the instinct which forever goads it to soar higher and higher.

In the best of Massinger's characters we seem to have a true, unconscious picture of himself, a photographic likeness, as it were, of his soul

---

* Carew. Epitaph on Lady Mary Villers.

when the sunshine was upon it. We mean in their speeches, for their actions are held in utter serfdom by the plot, which Massinger seems to have considered sovereign by divine right. To change their entire nature seems but a light exercise of their loyalty, and they would drink up Eysell or eat a crocodile for the gratification of their liege lord with pleased alacrity. There is but little variety in his leading characters, and they are all plainly Philip Massinger. It has often been said that the greatest genius never thus reproduces itself. Byron felt this to be true, as is clear from the uneasiness he showed when the masks of his various characters were torn away and disclosed beneath the narrow features of the peer. The true test seems to us the sameness rather than the portraiture of self, for genius must draw from within, and it differs from other natures not in being of a higher kind but in that it contains all others. *   Which of

---

*   .   .   .   only spirit
In whom the tempers and the minds of all
Should be shut up.
Shakespeare. Troilus and Cresida, A. **1**, S. **3**.

Shakespeare's characters shall we say is Shakespeare?—and yet, which shall we say is not? Round the brow of all Byron's heroes we can trace a scarlet token of the pressure of a coronet. That little imaginary golden circle had ample room and verge enough for the poet's soul;—what, save the emblem of eternity, could have been a proper fillet for that of Shakespeare?

To return to Massinger. There is a great deal of nobleness about him, and often we catch the lingering savour of a rich and fearless benignity which had been driven from its still home in his heart by the hard and bitter uses of the world. His nobleness is clearly his own, and not an outside virtue put on with his player's cloak and left in the wardrobe of the theatre folded up for fear of soiling. We say his nobleness is his own,—for there is a nobleness which is not noble, a fair-weather greatness, springing from without, whereby a man is wafted to honourable deeds by the prosperous breath of friends' applause, or is spurred on thereto by a pitiful emulation of the laurels rather than of

the nature of a true, inborn worthiness.   Nobleness emulates itself only, and shows as majestic
in its own sight as in that of the world.   It is
humble enough to think God as good society as
man.   We do not mean that the glorified lives
and deaths of the great souls who have gone before it are not to be a staff and a help to the
noble spirit, but we deem that but a bastard
greatness which must take root in the past, fearing to trust its seeds to the dim future, and pre-
ferring the beggarly Outward to the infinite
Within.   It is out of this meagre soil that the
desire of fame springs, which has never yet
achieved aught for the advancement of the race,
and which seems rather to be a quality of the
body than of the soul.   The soul is put here to
purify and elevate itself, and thereby the universal soul of man ; and it needs no outward
token of reverence, since it carries with it an
inward record and badge of its having fulfilled
its mission, more authentic than the palm branch
of the pilgrim to Jerusalem, or the green turban
of the Hadgi.   But the body, having more sym-

pathies with the earth than with heaven, is forever haunted by a longing to leave behind it
here some ponderous marble satire upon the
shortcomings of its former tenant. The true
poet feels nothing of this. Like his mother
Nature, he casts down his seeds with a free and
bounteous hand, and leaves them to the nursing
of the sun and the rain, the wind and the dew.
Massinger is clearly of a natively honourable and
fair composition. He is one of those who could
not help being noble, even if littleness were the
whole world's ideal of beauty. His greatness
was domestic wholly, and did not lean upon
others. For what true Man asks the verdict of
any soul but his own ? Simple, self-forgetting
majesty is one great charm of these old poets.
It was natural and homely, and thought not of
the reviews or the market-place. Its root is inward, but it blossoms and bears fruit outwardly
in deeds and words of a lofty and godlike justice
and simplicity. But for that other bastard
usurping virtue, as its root is outward, would
that its blossoms and fruit might be outward

likewise, and so the soul be free from unsatisfied longings, from the gnawings of reproachful seeming, and all other craven terrors.

One chief cause of the higher grandeur of the poesy of those days was that poets reverenced their calling, and did not lightly assume the holy name of seer—a name which, for some generations since, seems to have been mainly claimed and most readily conceded to those who could *not* see, so that what was once the type of all most awful and majestic things became a mock and a byeword, and those golden arrows which had slain the Pythian serpent and whose dreadful clang had sent fear through the bravest hearts of Greece, were either defiled and bedimmed by the foul venom of a crawling satire, or, reeking with wine, and feathered with courtly ribaldry, were launched feebly from the stews and bagnios at the hearts of Celias and Cloes whose arcadia was the court of Charles II, and their *Astraea redux*, the Duchess of Portsmouth. Our elder poets did so much talk of living *for* eternity as think of living *in* it, well knowing that time is not a

point without it, but that now and in the soul
of man is indeed the very centre on which that
infinite circle can alone be described. In those
days even the quacks had loftier ideas of their
art and of the nobleness of life requisite to its
practisers than many a poet now has of his. *

Massinger had a true and lofty feeling of the
sacred calling of the poet. He thought rather
of what he was born for than of himself. For,
inasmuch as the poetic nature is more truly and
fully expressed in a man, by so much is there
less of individuality and personality about him.
This nature exists in its highest and clearest
beauty where the spirit of the man is wholly
given up to the universal spirit, and the seer feels

---

* Lilly, the astrologer, who sat for the portrait of Sidrophel in
Hudibras, speaking of astrology, says "the study required in that
kind of learning must be sedentary, of great reading, sound judgment, which no man can accomplish except he wholly retire, use
prayer, *and accompany himself with angelical visitations.*—(*See his
Autobiography.*) So also Michael Sandivogius, in his New
Light of Alchymy, says "The searcher of Nature ought to be
such as Nature herself is, true, plain, patient, constant; and that
which is chiefest of all, religious, fearing God, not injurious to their
neighbour."

himself to be only the voice of something beyond thought and more sure than reason,—something more awful and mysterious than can be arrived at by the uttermost gropings of the most unbounded and strongest-winged imagining. Somewhat lower than this, but in the same kind, is Art, which seems, after all definitions, to be merely the unconscious instinct of genius, that is—of the healthiest and most natural nature.* Thus, in the hand of the true artist, the pen, the brush, or the chisel, seems rather to be in the all-powerful grasp of destiny herself, with so much swiftness and easy certainty does it body forth such baser and more outward portions of the overruling beauty as may be materially expressed, creating for the philosopher *proofs* † of those universal laws which he is laboriously splicing out of separate facts.   Only in the

---

* Sir Thomas Browne calls "art the perfection of nature," and "nature the art of God."—*Religio Medici.*

† Coleridge, hearing one speak of an argument between Mackintosh and somebody else which had been very long and intricate, exclaimed "If there had been a man of genius in the room he would have settled it in five minutes."—*Hazlitt's Remains.*

rapid flush of inspiration,—in the highest moments of the highest souls,—is this perfect artistic unconsciousness attained to by man, for the spirit of God cannot flow through these channels of clay, without losing somewhat of its crystal clearnesss.

We have said that Massinger's attempts at humour generally sank into grossness. There was no luxuriance in his character. He has none of that spiritual sensuousness which we so often find connected with the highest poetic faculty—a kind of rosy nakedness of Greek freedom which yet has no touch of immodesty in it. It is a faculty which belongs in perfection only to that evenly-balanced nature which gives its just right to both body and soul. It is as far removed from sensuality as from over delicacy, which may be called conventionalized grossness, since it keeps indeed its eyes and lips chaste as the icicle that hangs in Dian's temple, but has its heart and fancy thronging with prophetic pictures of all manner of uncleanliness which may by any remote chance assail it.

There is less immodesty in the stark nakedness
of virtue than in the closest veil of vice.

Massinger has grossness enough, but none of
this fine sensuality—this *bodily feeling* of the
beautiful. Indeed, it is inconsistent with grossness, being but an entire fusion of body and
spirit, so that we hear, see, smell, touch, and
taste, with the soul. It is a lifting of the body
up to the soul's level, whereas grossness brings
down the soul to that of the body. Poets who
possess this instinct most fully are the best de-
scribers of outward and material nature, with
which, through their bodily senses thus sub-
limated, they have a finer and wider sympathy.
And it is not by going out of themselves into
nature that they can, as it were, paint the very
feelings of seemingly dead and senseless things,
but rather by taking her into and interpenetrat-
ing her with their own spirits, thus showing the
true law of sympathy, which is to raise its ob-
jects to its own fullest height, and not to de-
scend to others. Therefore in the best land-
scapes, even of the most desert and barren

solitudes, the crowning charm seems to be a
certain humanness which sympathizes with the
highest wants of the soul, and has like feelings,
as it may be, of the sunlight and moonlight and
all the vast harmonies of Nature. We did not
look to find this faculty in Massinger. It has
only been shown by our greatest poets. We
find it in Chaucer, Spenser, and Shakespeare
eminently, and in our own day perhaps more in
Keats than any other. Sometimes we see it
reversed, and find the spirit sensualized, as in
some of the poems of Crashawe, a man of impure youth and Magdalen age, by whom the
marriage of the soul with the Saviour is cele-
brated in strains better befitting an earthly Epi-
thalamium.

Massinger's style is manly, strong, and straightforward. He writes blank-verse remarkably
well for a man whose lyrics and other attempts
at rhyme prove him to have been entirely desti-
tute of any musical ear. Sometimes, when he
imitates the favourite trick of Fletcher, and ends
his lines with what may be termed a spondee,

his verse has a show of more grace than is usual
with him. As in the two following passages
which have moreover a great tenderness of
sentiment.

> Good madam, for your health's sake, clear these clouds up
> That feed upon your beauty like diseases.
> Time's hand will turn again, and what he ruins
> Gently restore, and wipe off all your sorrows.
> Believe, you are to blame, much to blame, lady;
> You tempt his loving care whose eye has numbered
> All our afflictions and the time to cure them:
> You rather with this torrent choke his mercies,
> Than gently slide into his providence.
> Sorrows are well allowed, and sweeten nature
> When they express no more than drops on lilies;
> But, when they fall in storms, they bruise our hopes,
> Make us unable, though our comforts meet us,
> To hold our heads up: come, you shall take comfort;
> This is a sullen grief becomes condemnèd men,
> That feel a weight of sorrow through their souls:
> Do but look up. Why, so! is not this better
> Than hanging down your head still like a violet
> And dropping out those sweet eyes for a wager?

In this passage, sixteen out of the nineteen
lines end in the manner indicated above. Again,

> Not far from where my father lives, a lady,
> A neighbour by, blest with as great a beauty
> As nature durst bestow without undoing,

Dwelt, and most happily, as I thought then,
And blest the house a thousand times she dwelt in.
This beauty, in the blossom of my youth,
When my first fire knew no adulterate incense,
Nor I no way to flatter but my fondness,
In all the bravery my friends could show me,
In all the faith mine innocence could give me,
In the best language my true tongue could tell me,
And all the broken sighs my sick heart lend me,
I sued and served. Long did I love this lady,
Long was my travail, long my trade to win her;
With all the duty of my soul I served her.

We now and then meet in his plays some of
those forced conceits which became so fashion-
able a short time after in the writings of what
has been (rather inaptly) called " the metaphy-
sical school," who would borrow the shears of
Atropos to snip off a flower of speech, and seem
to have taken more pains to " cast a figure "
than ever astrologers did. We copy one
specimen.

My much loved lord, were Margaret only fair,
The cannon of her more than earthly form,
Though mounted high, commanding all beneath it,
And rammed with bullets of her sparkling eyes,
Of all the bulwarks that defend your senses
Could batter none but that which guards your sight.

This is as bad as some of the gallant Wyatt's sonnets, or as that prison which King Thibaud the troubadour tells us he was locked in " of which Love keeps the key, aided by his three bailiffs Hope Deferred, Beauty, and Anxiety." Chapman sometimes indulges his fancy in the same way; but in him it seems. like the play of a giant heaping Ossa on Pelion. Butler, a man of genius and sturdy English feeling, was wont to say, Aubrey tells us, that " that way (e. g. Edm. Waller's) of quibling with sence will hereafter growe as much out of fashion and be as ridicule as quibling with wordes." If all English poets had maintained their loyalty to our glorious tongue as fearlessly as Butler did * and had not so sheepishly allowed half-penny critics to be the best judges of an art as far above them as the glorious lyre which nightly burns in Heaven, our "collections of Poets" would not have been so much like catacombs of withered anatomies, which fall to dust under our touch.

---

* See his poems " On Critics," and "On Our ridiculous imitation of the French " in especial.

We finish our extracts with the following from "The Roman Actor," which shews that Massinger had a true feeling of the independence of the poet and of the stage, and that he esteemed the latter (what it doubtless is when rightly conducted) a good helper in the cause of virtue and refinement.

> .   .   .   But, 'tis urged
> That we corrupt youth, and traduce superiors :—
> When do we bring a vice upon the stage
> That does go off unpunished ?   Do we teach,
> By the success of wicked undertakings,
> Others to tread in their forbidden steps ?
> We show no arts of Lydian panderism,
> Corinthian poisons, Persian flatteries,
> But mulcted so in the conclusion, that
> Even those spectators that were so inclined
> Go home changed men.   And, for traducing such
> That are above us, publishing to the world
> Their secret crimes, we are as innocent
> As such as are born dumb.   When we present
> An heir that does conspire against the life
> Of his dear parent, numbering every hour
> He lives as tedious to him ; if there be
> Among the auditors one whose conscience tells him
> He is of the same mould,—WE CANNOT HELP IT.
> Or, bringing on the stage a loose adulteress,
> That does maintain the riotous expense

Of him that feeds her greedy lust, yet suffers
The lawful pledges of a former bed
To starve the while for hunger ; if a matron,
However great in fortune, birth, or titles
Guilty of such a foul, unnatural sin,
Cry out—'t is writ for me,—WE CANNOT HELP IT.
Or, when a covetous man's exprest, whose wealth
Arithmetic cannot number, and whose lordships
A falcon in one day cannot fly over,
Yet he so sordid in his mind, so griping,
As not to afford himself the necessaries
To maintain life ;—if a patrician
(Though honoured with a consulship) find himself
Touched to the quick in this,—WE CANNOT HELP IT.
Or, when we show a judge that is corrupt
And will give up the sentence, as he favours
The person not the cause, saving the guilty,
If of his faction, and as oft condemning
The innocent out of particular spleen,—
If any in this reverend assembly,
Nay, even yourself, my lord, that are the image
Of absent Cæsar, feel something in your bosom
That puts you in remembrance of things past
Or things intended,—'T IS NOT IN US TO HELP IT.

And so, farewell, Philip Massinger!—Thou wast one of the deathless brotherhood who reared so fair a statue to the god of song, for the love and reverence ye bore him only, and not like Domitian, that your own images might show

prominently on his bosom.   Happy art thou now
in thy nameless grave, free from the cark and care
whose bitter rust prey most upon the poet's heart.
Happy in that thou canst be praised without
envy, and that thou art far removed from the
carping of men who would measure all genius by
their standard,—who respect the dead body more
than the living soul, and who esteem contempo-
raneousness an excuse for malignity, grossness,
and all other basenesses, which disgracefully dis-
tinguish the man from the brute.   Happy art
thou there in the infinite peace and silence.

The Plays of ❦ ❦ Thomas Middleton

A great poem is a fountain for ever, overflowing with the waters of wisdom and delight, and after one person and one age have exhausted all of its divine influence which their peculiar relations enable them to share, another and yet another succeeds, and new relations are ever developed, the source of an unforeseen and unconceived delight.

—Shelly's Defense of Poetry

POETS are the forerunners and prophets of changes in the moral world. Driven, by their fine nature, to search into and reverently contemplate the universal laws of soul, they find some fragment of the broken tables of God's laws, and interpret it, half conscious of its mighty import. While philosophers are wrangling, and politicians playing at snapdragon with the destinies of millions, the poet, in the silent deeps of his soul listens to those mysterious pulses which, from one central heart, send life and beauty through the finest veins of the universe, and utters truth to be sneered at, perchance, by contemporaries, but which become religion to posterity. Not unwisely ordered is that eternal destiny which renders the seer despised of men, since thereby he is but the more surely taught to lay his head meekly upon the mother-breast of Nature, and hearken to the musical soft beating of her bounteous heart.

That Poesy, save as she can soar nearer to the blissful throne of the Supreme Beauty, is

of no more use than all other beautiful things
are, we are fain to grant. That she does not
add to the outward wealth of the body, and that
she is only so much more excellent than any bodily
gift, as spirit is more excellent than matter, we
must also yield. But, inasmuch as all beautiful
things are direct messages and revelations of himself, given us by our Father, and as Poesy is the
searcher out and interpreter of all these, tracing
by her inborn sympathy the invisible nerves
which bind them harmoniously together, she is
to be revered and cherished. The poet has a
fresher memory of Eden, and of the path leading back thereto, than other men; so that we
might almost deem him to have been conceived,
at least, if not born and nursed, beneath the am-
brosial shadow of those dimly remembered bow-
ers, and to have had his infant ears filled with
the divine converse of angels, who then talked
face to face with his sires, as with beloved
younger brethren, and of whose golden words
only the music remained to him, vibrating for
ever in his soul, and making him yearn to have

all sounds of earth harmonize therewith.   In the poet's lofty heart Truth hangs her aery, and there Love flowers, scattering thence her winged seeds over all the earth with every wind of heaven.   In all ages the poet's fiery words have goaded men to remember and regain their ancient freedom, and, when they had regained it, have tempered it with a love of beauty, so as that it should accord with the freedom of Nature, and be as unmovably eternal as that.   The dreams of poets are morning-dreams, coming to them in the early dawn and day-breaking of great truths, and are surely fulfilled at last.   They repeat them, as children do, and all Christendom, if it be not too busy with quarrelling about the meaning of creeds, which have no meaning at all, listens with a shrug of the shoulders and a smile of pitying incredulity ; for reformers are always madmen in their own age, and infallible saints in the next.

We love to go back to the writings of our old poets, for we find in them the tender germs of many a thought which now stands like a huge

oak in the inward world, an ornament and a
shelter. We cannot help reading with awful interest what has been written or rudely scrawled
upon the walls of this our earthly prison-house,
by former dwellers therein. From that which
centuries have established, too, we may draw
true principles of judgment for the poetry of our
own day. A right knowledge and apprehension
of the past teaches humbleness and self-sustain-
ment to the present. Showing us what has been,
it also reveals what can be done. Progress is
Janus-faced, looking to the bygone as well as to
the coming; and Radicalism should not so much
busy itself with lopping off the dead or seeming
dead limbs, as with clearing away that poisonous
rottenness around the roots, from which the tree
has drawn the principle of death into its sap.
A love of the beautiful and harmonious, which
must be the guide and forerunner to every onward movement of humanity, is created and
cherished more surely by pointing out what
beauty dwells in anything, even the most deformed, (for there is something in that, also, else

it could not even *be*,) than by searching out and
railing at all the foulness in nature.   Not till we
have patiently studied beauty can we safely venture to look at defects, for not till then can we
do it in that spirit of earnest love, which gives
more than it takes away.   Exultingly as we hail
all signs of progress, we venerate the past also.
The tendrils of the heart, like those of ivy, cling
but the more closely to what they have clung to
long, and even when that which they entwine
crumbles beneath them, they still run greenly
over the ruin, and beautify those defects which
they cannot hide.   The past, as well as the
present, moulds the future, and the features of
some remote progenitor will revive again freshly
in the latest offspring of the womb of time.
Our earth hangs well-nigh silent now, amid the
chorus of her sister orbs, and not till past and
present move harmoniously together will music
once more vibrate on this long silent chord in
the symphony of the universe.

Of Thomas Middleton little is known.   Indeed, it seems to be the destiny of poets that

men should not be familiar with their personal
history—a destiny which to the thoughtful has
a true and beautiful meaning. For it seems
meant to chide men for their too ready preference
of names and persons to *things*, by showing them
the perishableness of the one and the immortality of the other, and to give to those divine
teachings of theirs which remain to us something of a mysterious and oracular majesty, as
if they were not truly the words of men, but
only more distant utterances of those far-heard
voices which, in the too fleeting moments of a
higher and clearer being, come to us from the
infinite deep with a feeling of something heard
in childhood, but long ago drowned in the din
of life. It is a lesson, also, for those who would
be teachers of men that theirs must be rather the
humbly obedient voice than the unconquerable
will, and that he speaks best who has listened longest. And yet there is something beautiful, too, in the universal longing which men feel
to see the bodily face of that soul whose words
have strengthened or refreshed them. It is, per-

haps, the result of an unconscious remembrance of a perished faith in the power of spirit over matter, whereby the beautiful soul builds for itself out of clay a dwelling worthy and typical of its majesty. Let Orpheus, then, be a shadow, Homer a name, and our divine Shakespeare a mystery;—we might despise the ambrosia if we saw too plainly the earthen dish in which it was offered to us. Their spirits are a part of the air we breathe. Nothing that was truly theirs has perished, or ever can perish. If a sparrow fall not to the ground without His knowledge, shall a word of truth be of less esteem in His eyes than a sparrow? No; buffeted and borne about as it may be, by the shifting winds of prejudice, that deathless seed always takes root in the warm bosom of the earth at last:—buried for centuries haply in the dark and dreary catacombs of superstition, the life is yet new and strong within it, and in God's good time it springs up and blossoms, in an age to which it was more needful than to that in which it was entombed.

It is of Middleton's tragedies chiefly that we shall speak, both because they are very fine ones, and because from them we can more safely draw an estimate of his character. A good tragedy is, perhaps, the hardest thing to write. Nothing is easier than to draw tears from the reader; nothing surely is more rare than the power of drawing them rightly, or of touching that deepest string of our being which God, that he might give us the most meaning lesson of universal brotherhood, has ordained should never quiver at the touch of our private sorrows, how soul-piercing soever. There are a thousand who can write pathetically, for one who has in any measure of fulness the tragic faculty. Many may touch the heart, but none save a master can bring up for us the snowy pearls which sleep in the deep abysses and caverns of the soul. That our tears are so ready has a beautiful significance,—for they are the birthright of angelic natures, while it is the curse of utterly fallen spirits that none of this sweet dew should ever shed its coolness upon their parched and burning cheeks. Viewed rightly, every fact of our being enfolds a clear recognition of the divinity of our nature. In childhood we see this more readily, though unwittingly;—every flower which we pluck at random in the pure morning of life, and cast from us with a prodigality of beauty which we grow charier of in more thoughtful years, circles in its fragrant heart the dew-drop which, small as it is, mirrors the universe. In childhood, too, and in women, (who never wander far thence,) the source of this never turbid fountain of our tears is nearer the surface. The drifting sands of a life, which our own selfishness makes a desert, slowly choke it as we grow older, till at last that which was once a gentle outlet of the crowded heart becomes in itself a more bitter agony. Beautiful, therefore, and blessed is the power of calling forth these pledges of a tenderest purity which lingers life-long, fluttering anear its scattered nest, and will not be scared away. How more beautiful and blessed it is so to summon them as that they shall give

back to us, though only for a moment, these
holy impulses and gracious instincts of which
they were once both the proof and fulfilment.

And this last belongs wholly to tragedy,—
wherein we weep rather for the universal than
the particular,—for the blight which we sometimes in madness think to fall *always* on the
purest aspiration and the tenderest faith,—for
that blindness and weakness which we find also
in our own hearts, ready at any moment to mis-
lead us into unconscious sin, or to give way,
(for in our greatest strength we are the readiest
to lean upon reeds,) and to plunge us headlong
and dizzy into the same dreary void with those
imaginary woes which so move us. But the
wounds which Nature gives us are always to
free us from some morbid humour; and, tragedy,
in proving to us the weakness of humanity,
shows us at the same time its glorious strength,
and that if lower, we are but a little lower than
the angels,—a majestic height, where we may
poise serenely, if we clog not our silver plumes
with clay. In tragedy, moreover, Destiny al-

ways hangs like a thunder-cloud, vague and
huge, upon the horizon, with an awful grandeur,
and we hear afar its ominous mutterings, and see
its lightning reflected on the blue craggy mass
which it reveals to us, hanging dimly over our
own heads. Shapes float around us and voices
are heard from another life, and we are awed
into an unwilling consciousness of the workings
of an unseen and inscrutable power. But in
writings strictly pathetic our sympathies are
moved either for the individual suffering, or
against the power (always a definite one) which
inflicts it unjustly. Pathos deals with the unnatural causes; tragedy with those mysterious
exceptions to the laws of nature which are no less
natural than those laws themselves with which
they make such seeming discord. Pathos is
wholly the more outward of the two; it may be
founded on the elegancies or conventionalities of
life, on the vices and wrongs of a wholly artificial system of society. But tragedy can only
take root in the deepest and most earnest realities of a nature common to us all, the same
Œdipus and Othello. The master of pathos

must be minute and circumstantial, he must tell us all he knows, and depend on a cumulative effect; while for the higher tragic there are many things too real and commonplace;—the naked skeleton, which leaves the imagination free to work, is more effective and apalling,—the undefinable shadow, whose presence we feel, but toward which we dare not turn our heads. Pathos clings close to the body, and death is one of its favourite and most moving themes. The interest of tragedy is one with life, and touches us through our sense of immortality. Tragedy has to do with the deepest and holiest part of our nature, and breathes over strings which echo dimly far away in the infinite and eternal. It lifts us above the pent-up horizon of the body, and unfolds us to wider and more spiritual relations, so that we wonder not when Prometheus calls upon the sea for sympathy, or when Lear finds a humanity in the elements, and in that grey heaven which, like himself, was full of years. Disease, poverty, death, which tears away from us the body of those whom we had loved,—that body round which our spirits had twined themselves, hiding it with their luxuriant leaves and tendrils, till we believed that it could not but partake somewhat of that deathless essence,—these and many more woes is our frail humanity incident to; but there are anguishes of our immortal nature deeper than life and death;—Laocoön struggles with the entwining fold of destiny, doubts that hurry to and fro in bewildered hopelessness,—loss of faith in good, and seemingly forced belief in an overruling evil, when Truth shows but as a painted mask over the stony face of Falsehood, when a damp mist of despair swathes the beautiful in its icy shroud, and Love, which we had deemed unchangeable, hides its eyes from us,—and these belong to Tragedy, which always shows us that the finite can never be an independent existence, but is ever overruled by the infinite, to which it is knit by unseen but never-to-be-sundered bands. To write a good tragedy, therefore, demands, if not the greatest of poets, certainly some of the highest elements of one.

The plot of " The Changeling," the most powerful of Middleton's tragedies, is briefly this. DeFlores, a deformed and ugly villain, loves Beatrice, the heroine of the play, who has an unconquerable loathing of him. She has been betrothed by Vermandero, her father, to Alonzo de Piracquo, a noble gentleman, but whom she cannot love, having already given all her heart to Alsemero. DeFlores first tempts her to the murder of Piracquo, and then offers himself as the instrument of that hideous guilt. The murder is successfully accomplished without the knowledge of Alsemero, and Beatrice, no obstacle now remaining, is married to him. On the day of her wedding she deems it high time to get DeFlores out of the way, but he refuses any other reward than the satiation of his hellish passion for Beatrice, to the gratification of which he compels her by a threat of disclosing all to her husband. Alsemero at length is led to suspect his wife, the whole ghastly story is laid bare, and DeFlores, after slaying his unwilling paramour, prevents the revenging steel of Tomaso, Piracquo's brother, by stabbing himself to the heart. The tragedy takes its name from the chief character in an under-plot, which, as is usually the case in the old drama, has nothing whatever to do with the action of the piece.

In the opening of the play, Beatrice thus strongly expresses her aversion to DeFlores:

> .   .   .   'Tis my infirmity ;
> Nor can I other reason render you
> Than his or hers of some particular thing
> They must abandon as a deadly poison,
> Which to a thousand other tastes were wholesome ;
> Such to mine eyes is that same fellow there,
> The same that report speaks of the basilisk.

It was a fine thought in our author thus to give a dim foreshadowing of that bloody eclipse of her better nature which Beatrice was to suffer from DeFlores. It is always an unacknowledged sense of our own weaknesses that gives birth to those vague feelings and presentiments which warn us of an approaching calamity, and when the blow has fallen, we soothe our wounded self-respect by calling it Fate. We cheat our sterner reason into a belief that some higher power has interfered to bring about that blight in us whose steady growth always circles outward from some hidden meanness in our own souls. Our woes are our own offspring, and

we feed our hungry brood, as was once fabled of
the pelican, with our best heart's blood;——alas!
they never become fledged, like hers, and fly
away from us, but raven till the troubled fountain runs dry! The shafts of destiny never
rend through buckler and breast-plate, but reach
our hearts with an awful and deadly certainty,
through any chink in our armour which has been
left unbraced by our own sin or recklessness.
Beatrice would make us believe that she has a
natural antipathy to DeFlores.   But antipathies
are only so many proofs of something wanting
in ourselves, whereby we are hindered of that
perfect sympathy with all things, for which we
were created, and without which that life, which
should be as harmonious as the soft consent of
love, becomes harsh and jarring.   The thought
of DeFlores is to Beatrice what the air-drawn
dagger was to Macbeth; she foresees in her own
heart the crime yet uncommitted, and trembles
at the weapon even while she stretches her quivering hand to grasp it.   A terrible fascination
seems to draw us on to the doing of ill deeds,
the foreconsciousness whereof, graciously im-

planted in our natures by God as a safeguard, we misconstrue into the promptings of our evil demon.   We brood over the gloomy thought in an agony of fierce enjoyment.   Infidels to our holy impulses, we blaspheme the eternal benignity which broods for ever on its chosen nest in the soul of man, giving life to all beauty and all strength.   We go apart from the society of men that we may hold converse with our self-invoked and self-created tempter.   Always at our backs it dogs us, looming every hour higher and higher, till the damp gloom of its shadow hems us wholly in.   We feel it behind us like the fearful presence of a huge hand stretched forth to grip us and force us to its withering will.   One by one the dark, vague fingers close around us, and at last we render ourselves to its fancied bidding in a gush of wild despair which vibrates within us with a horrid delight.*

* We need only refer to the masterly illustration of this thought in Mr. Dana's "Paul Felton," a tale of wonderful depth and power.   The spiritual meaning of the witches in Macbeth is doubtless this tempering of a soul with its warnings against, which it mistakes for ominous suggestions to, evil.

We sign our deeds of sale to the fiend with a feather self-torn from our own wings. It is the curse of Adam in us that we can no longer interpret the tongue of angels, and too often mistake the tender forethought of our good spirit concerning us, for the foul promptings of an evil demon which we would fain believe is permitted to have dominion over us. In another place Beatrice says to DeFlores:

> *I never see this fellow but I think*
> *Of some harm towards me; danger's in my mind still;*
> *I scarce leave trembling for an hour after.*

Here we have a still clearer omen of what is to follow.

Our poet drops a few " lilies in the mouth of his Tartarus," but there is ever a dark sprig of nightshade among them. In the scene we next quote, the bloody dawning of the thought of Piracquo's murder in the soul of Beatrice blots out luridly the tender morning-star of love which still trembles there, making us feel yet more thrillingly the swiftly nearing horrors which it betokens. The scene is between Beatrice and Alsemero.

Beat. I have within mine eyes all my desires:
Requests, that holy prayers ascend heaven for,
And bring them down to furnish our defects,
Come not more sweet to our necessities
Than thou unto my wishes.

Als. We are so like
In our expressions, lady, that unless I borrow
The same words, I shall never find their equals.

Beat. How happy were this meeting, this embrace,
If it were free from envy—this poor kiss,
It has an enemy, a hateful one,
That wishes poison to it: how well were I now,
If there were none such name known as Piracquo,
Nor no such tie as the command of parents!
I should be too much blessed.

Als. One good service
Would strike off both your fears, and I'll go near it, too,
Since you are so distressed, remove the cause,
The command ceases; so there's two fears blown out
With one and the same blast.

Beat. Pray, let me find you, sir:
What might that service be, so strangely happy?

Als. The honourablest piece about man, valour;
I'll send a challenge to Piracquo instantly.

With what exquisite naturalness is this drawn !
The heart of Beatrice, afraid of itself, would fain
cheat itself into the belief that Alsemero gave it
that dark hint which its own guilty wishes had
already forestalled.   To return—

Beat. How ? call you that extinguishing of fear,
When 't is the only way to keep it flaming?
Are not you ventured in the action,
That 's all my joys and comforts ? pray, no more, sir:

Though she seemingly rejects the offer, yet she goes on weighing the risk in her own mind.

Say you 've prevailed, you're danger's and not mine then ;
The law would claim you from me, or obscurity
Be made the grave to bury you alive.
I'm glad these thoughts came forth; oh, keep not one
Of this condition, sir ! here was a course
Found to bring sorrow on her way to death ;
The tears would ne'er have dried till dust had choked them.
Blood-guiltiness becomes a fouler visage;————

Thus she works herself up to a pitch of horror at the fancied guilt of Alsemero, and with half-conscious cunning renders her own plot, (which she now for the first time acknowledges to herself,) less full of loathsomeness. She continues (*aside*):

And now I think on one; I was to blame,
I've marred so good a market with my scorn;
It had been done, questionless: the ugliest creature
Creation framed for some use; yet to see
I could not mark so much where it should be!

How full of doubt and trembling hesitation is the broken structure of the verse, too, and how

true to nature the lie in the last line and a half,
which she will persist in telling herself.

> *Als.* Lady——

But she does not hear him; she is too fearfully
intent with watching a murder even now adoing
in her own heart.

> *Beat.* (*aside*).   Why, men of art make much of poison,
> Keep one to expel another; where was my art?

The scene which follows, between Beatrice
and DeFlores, is a very powerful one.   Not
powerful in the same degree as Lear and Othello,
but yet in the same kind, for as much power is
needful to the making of a violet as of an oak.
It is too long for us to copy the whole of it.   She
tries to persuade herself that DeFlores is not so
hideous to her after all, like a child talking aloud
in the dark to relieve its terrors.

> When we are used
> To a hard face it is not so unpleasing;
> It mends still in opinion, hourly mends,
> I see it by experience.   .   .   .   .   .
> Hardness becomes the visage of a man well;
> It argues service, resolution, manhood,
> If cause were of employment.

DeFlores is led on gradually to the desired end,
and when he has sworn to devote himself to

whatever service she may lay upon him, she exclaims, not daring to hear the name of "her murdered man" on her lips till emboldened by slow degrees :

> Then take *him* to thy fury!
> *DeF.*   I thirst for him!
> *Beat.*   Alonzo de Piracquo!

DeFlores murders Piracquo, and brings one of his fingers, with a ring upon it, as a token of the deed to Beatrice.   She is startled at sight of him.

> *Beat.*   DeFlores!
> *DeF.*   Lady?

She will not trust her tongue with anything more than an allusion to what she so eagerly longed for.

> *Beat.*   Thy looks promise cheerfully.
> *DeF.*   All things are answerable, time, circumstance,
> Your wishes, and my service.
> *Beat.*   Is IT done, then?
> *DeF.*   Piracquo is no more.
> *Beat.*   My joys start at mine eyes; *our sweet'st delights*
> *Are evermore born weeping.*
> *DeF.*   I have a token for you.
> *Beat.*   For me ?
> *DeF.*   But it was sent somewhat unwillingly:
> I could not get the ring without the finger.
> *Beat.*   Bless me, what hast thou done!—

exclaims the horror-stricken Beatrice, the woman reviving again in her. She had hardened herself to the abstract idea of murder, but revolts at this dreadful material token of it.

> *DeF.* Why, is that more
> Than killing the whole man? I cut his heart-strings.

How finely is the contemptuous coolness of DeFlores, the villain by calculation, set off by the shrinking dread of Beatrice, whose guilt is the child of a ravished intercourse between her passions and her affections. The sight of the ring carries her and us back to the sweet days of her innocency, and the picture is complete.

> 'T is the first token my father made me send him.

She sighs, remembering the calm purity from which she has fallen, and yet, at the same time, with the true cunning of guiltiness which only half repents, strives to palliate the sin of whose terrible consciousness she must evermore be the cringing bondslave, by thinking of her father's tyranny. The horror which a murderer feels at the *physical fact* of murder and the dread which creeps over him from the cold corpse of his victim, exemplified by Beatrice in the above

quotation, seem, at first thought, strange pheno—
mena in nature.   But are they not in truth un-
witting recognitions of the immortality of the
soul, as if the wrong done were wholly to the
body, and had no terrors for the spiritual part of
our being?   This feeling may be well called
bodily remorse, being clearly of a grosser and more
outward nature than that strong agony which
shakes us inwardly when we have done a murder
upon the soul of our brother, and have been
marked on our foreheads as spiritual Cains, by
ingratitude, hypocrisy, mistrust, want of faith, or
any other lie against God.*

The remainder of this scene between De-
Flores and Beatrice is all of it striking, but we
have not room to quote it all.   DeFlores tells
her the loathsome price at which she has bought
Piracquo's death, and she exclaims:

> Why 't is impossible thou canst be so wicked,
> Or shelter such a cunning cruelty,
> To make his death the murderer of my honour!

---

* This bodily feeling is painted with a terrible truth and distinct-
ness of colouring in Hood's " Dream of Eugene Aram," and with
no less strength by the powerful imagination of Mr. Poe, in his
story of the " Tell-Tale Heart."

Thy language is so bold and vicious,
I cannot see which way I can forgive it
With any modesty.

No guilt can ever sear out of a woman's soul the essential tenderness and purity of its nature. Desecrated as its dwelling may be by infamy and shame, with meek and silent forgiveness it comes home again to its ruined cell, and gently effaces, as far as it can, the ruthless traces of the destroyer. Alas! where the celestial whiteness of woman's nature is most bedimmed, she stands most in need of the uplifting sympathy of her sisters, who only give her scorn or a distant pity, which makes her but the more an outcast. How more ennobling and worthy of us it is to seek out and cherish the soiled remnant of an angelic nature in the lepers of sin against whom the hard world has shut its iron doors, than to worship it (which we are not over-ready to do) where it shines unclouded in the noble and the wise.

This modesty of Beatrice is one of the most touchingly natural traits in her character. De-Flores spurned it as he would a worthless flower.

Pish! you forget yourself;
A woman dipped in blood and talk of modesty!

 Beat. O, misery of sin! would I'd been bound
Perpetually unto my living hate
In that Piracquo than to hear these words!
Think but upon the distance that creation
Set 'twixt thy blood and mine, and keep thee there.

She shrinks behind her pride, but the next
speech of DeFlores drives her forth from her
flimsy shelter. The speech is a very vigorous
one and full of moral truth.

 DeF. Look but into your conscience, read me there,
'T is a true book; *you'll find me there your equal:*
Pish! fly not to your birth, but settle you
In *what the act has made you, you're no more now;*
You must forget your parentage to me;
You are the deed's creature; by that name
You lost your first condition, *and I challenge you,*
As peace and innocency have turned you out,
And made you one with me.

 Beat. With thee, foul villain?

 DeF. Yes, my fair murderess, do you urge me?

Yes, there are no bounds of caste, no grades
of rank, in sin. If we may be born again in
virtue, so also may we be in sin, and we bear
some trace of the hideous features of our second
mother to our grave.

A very striking and forcible line is put into
the mouth of DeFlores when he first meets
Tomaso, Piracquo's brother, after the murder.

I 'd fain get off, this man 's not for my company,
I smell his brother's blood when I come near him.

Tom. Come hither, kind and true one ; I remember
My brother loved thee well.

DeF. O, purely, dear sir!
Methinks I'm now again akilling him,
He brings it so fresh to me. (*Aside*)

In another scene between Beatrice and
DeFlores she is made to say something which is
full of touching pathos. She suspects her maid
of having betrayed her to her husband. DeFlores
asks,

Who would trust a waiting-woman ?
Beat. *I must trust somebody.*

How truly is here expressed the wilderness of
bleak loneliness into which guilt drives those it
possesses, forcing them, when that sweet spring
of peacefulness, which bubbles up so freshly in
the open confidingness of joy, is cut off, to seek
sympathy in their degradation, and in the bewil-
dering darkness of doubt and suspicion to *trust*
some one, even though it be only with the story

of their shame.   In its lowest and most fallen
estate, the spirit of man cannot shake off its inborn feeling of brotherhood, which whispers to
it to seek that for sympathy which in happier
days it was perhaps too slow to grant.   It is
sorrow which teaches us most nearly how full of
sustainment and help we may be to our fellows,
and how much we in our turn stand in need of
them; and that when once selfishness has rusted
apart that chain which binds us so closely to
man, it has also broken the sustaining tie which
links us with uplifting trustfulness to the all-
enfolding sympathy of God.

In the last act Beatrice confesses her crime to
her husband, and he cries bitterly :

> O, thou art all deformed !
>   *Beat.*   Forget not, sir,
> It for your sake was done ; shall greater dangers
> Make thee less welcome ?
>   *Als.*   *O, thou should 'st have gone*
> *A thousand leagues about to have avoided*
> *This dangerous bridge of blood !*   Here we are lost !

There is a sternly truthful naturalness in these
words of Alsemero.   To a soul highly wrought
up, language resolves itself into its original ele-

ments, and the relations and resemblances of
things present themselves to it rather than the
things themselves, so that the language of passion,
in which conventionality is overwhelmed by the
bursting forth of the original savage nature is
always metaphorical. *

The tragic depth of the climax of this drama
can only be thoroughly felt in a perusal of the
whole. We can only quote a few sentences.
There is much pathos in what the broken-
hearted Beatrice says to her father, as she is
dying.

> O, come not near me, sir, I shall defile you !
> I am that of your blood was taken from you
> For your better health ; look no more upon it,
> But cast it to the ground regardlessly,
> Let the common sewer take it from distinction,
> Beneath the stars, upon yon meteor
> Ever hung my fate, 'mongst things corruptible ;
> (Pointing to DeFlores)
> I ne'er could pluck it from him ; my loathing
> Was prophet to the rest, but ne'er believed :
> Mine honour fell with him, and now my life.

* Coleridge's eloquent reasoning in opposition to this theory never
seemed to us at all satisfactory, and the very instances he adduces
are, to our mind, against him. See his " Apologetic Preface,"
which, however unconvincing, is certainly a magnificent specimen
of acute and thorough analysis.

The concluding words of the play with which Alsemero addresses his bereaved father-in-law are fragrant with beautiful and sincere humanity.

> Sir, you have yet a son's duty living,
> Please you, accept it ; let that your sorrow,
> As it goes from your eye, go from your heart ;
> Man and his sorrow at the grave must part.
> All we can do to comfort one another,
> To stay a brother's sorrow for a brother,
> To dry a child from a kind father's eyes,
> It is to no purpose, it rather multiplies :
> Your only smiles have power to cause re-live
> The dead again, or in their rooms to give
> Brother a new brother, father a child ;
> If these appear, all griefs are reconciled.

The dramatic power of Middleton is rather of the suggestive kind than of that elaborately minute and finished order, which can trust wholly to its own completeness for effect. Only Shakespeare can so " on horror's head horrors accumulate " as to make the o'ercharged heart stand aghast and turn back with trembling haste from the drear abyss in which it was groping bewildered. Middleton has shown his deep knowledge of art and nature by that strict appreciation of his own weakness, which is the hardest wisdom to gain, and which can only be the fruit of an earnest, willing, and humble study in his own heart, of those primitive laws of spirit which lie at the bottom of all hearts. It is much easier to feel our own strength than our want of it; indeed, a feeling of the one blinds us to the other. Middleton is wise in choosing rather to give mysterious hints which the mind may follow out, than to strive to lead the imagination, which is most powerful in conjuring up images of horror, beyond where he could guide it with bold and unwavering certainty. With electric sympathy we feel the bewilderment of our guide's mind through the hand with which he leads us, and refuse to go further, when, if left to ourselves, our very doubt would have enticed us onward.

To show our author's more graceful and delicate powers, we copy the following from another tragedy :

> How near am I now to a happiness
> The earth exceeds not ! not another like it;
> The treasures of the deep are not so precious
> As the concealed comforts of man
> Locked up in woman's love.   I scent the air

Of blessings when I come but near the house :
What a delicious breath marriage sends forth !
The violet-bed 's not sweeter.   Honest wedlock
Is like a banqueting house built in a garden
On which the spring's chaste flowers take delight
To cast their modest odours ; when base lust
With all her powders, paintings, and best pride,
Is but a fair house built by a ditch side.
.   .   .   Now for a welcome
Able to draw men's envies upon man ;
A kiss now that shall hang upon my lip
As sweet as morning dew upon a rose,
And full as long.

Another from the same play :

O, hast thou left me, then, Bianca, utterly ?
Bianca, now I miss thee !   O, return
And save the faith of woman !   I ne'er felt
The loss of thee till now; 't is an affliction
Of greater weight than youth was made to bear;
As if a punishment of after-life
Were fallen upon man here, so new it is
To flesh and blood so strange, so insupportable!
.   .   .   Canst thou forget
The dear pains my love took? how it was watched
Whole nights together, in all weathers, for thee,
Yet stood in heart more merry than the tempest
That sung about mine ears ?

We shall copy a few scattered passages and conclude :

THE SINS OF GREAT MEN

Every sin thou commit'st shows like a flame
Upon a mountain ; 't is seen far about,
And, with a big wind made of popular breath,
The sparkles fly through cities ; here one takes,
Another catches there, and in short time,
Waste all to cinders.

Our author's aptness in comparison is striking. He says of the shameful deed of a great man :

Great men are never sound men after it,
It leaves some ache or other in their names still,
Which their posterity feels at every weather.

CHARITY

You should love those you are not tied to love ;
That 's the right trial of a woman's charity.

HONOUR

The fame that a man wins himself is best ;
That he may call his own. Honours put to him
Make him no more a man than his clothes do,
And are as soon ta'en off.

WANT OF NOBLENESS

O, what vile prisons
Make we our bodies to our immortal souls !

SENSE OF GUILT

Still my adulterous guilt hovers aloft,
And with her black wings beats down all my prayers
Ere they be half-way up.

PRUDENCE

Wisely to fear is to be free from fear.

PATIENCE

Patience, my lord: why, 't is the soul of peace;
Of all the virtues 't is the nearest kin to heaven;
It makes men look like gods. The best of men
That e'er wore earth about him was a sufferer,
A soft, meek, patient, humble, tranquil spirit,
The first true gentleman that ever breathed.
The stock of patience then cannot be poor,
All it desires it has; what monarch more?

    .   .   .   .   .

'T is the perpetual prisoner's liberty,
His walks and orchards; 't is the bond-slave's freedom,
And makes him seem proud of each iron chain
As though he wore it more for state than pain;
It is the beggar's music, and thus sings,
Although our bodies beg our souls are kings!
O, my dread liege, it is the sap of bliss,
Rears us aloft, *makes men and angels kiss.*

A HAPPY MAN

He that in his coffin is richer than before,
He that counts youth his sword and age his staff,
He whose right hand carves his own epitaph.

Here is the sweetest description of the passage
of time, expressed by an outward reference, that
we recollect ever to have seen :

The moon hath *through her bow scarce drawn to the head,*
Like to twelve silver arrows, all the months,
Since,——

TWILIGHT

I come, dear love,
To take my last farewell, fitting this hour,
Which nor bright day will claim, nor pitchy night,
An hour fit to part conjoinèd souls.

THE WORLD

Stoop thou to the world, 't will on thy bosom tread ;
It stoops to thee if thou advance thy head.

The following is a revelation of the spiritual world, full of truth and beauty. Men whose material part predominates in them are afraid of spirits; but a *body* walking the earth after its heavenly tenant has left it is a more awful sight to spiritual minds.

My son was dead ; whoe'er outlives his virtues
Is a dead man ; for when you hear of spirits
That walk in real bodies, to the amaze
And cold astonishment of such as meet them,
.   .   .   those are men of vices,
Who nothing have but what is visible,
And so, by consequence, they have no souls.

THE BODY

There's but this wall betwixt you and destruction,
When you are at strongest, and but poor thin clay.

OVER-CUNNING

Grow not too cunning for your soul, good brother.

There is a simplicity and manly directness in our old writers of tragedy, which comes to us with the more freshness in a time so conventional as our own. In their day, if the barrier between castes was more marked than it is now, that between hearts was less so. They were seers, indeed, using reverently that rare gift of inward sight which God had blessed them with, and not daring to blaspheme the divinity of Beauty by writing of what they had not seen and truly felt in their own hearts and lives. It is one of the refinements of a more modern school which teaches artists to *open their mouths and shut their eyes*, as children are playfully told to, and wait for some mysterious power *to make them wise*. They wrote from warm, beating hearts, not from a pitiful, dry pericardium of fashion or taste, " formed after the purest models." They became worthy to lead, by having too much faith in nature to follow any but her. We find in them lessons for to-day, as fresh as when they were spoken, showing us that poetry is true for ever; that the spiritual presences which haunted their lonely hours with images of beauty

and precious inward promptings to truth and
love still walk the earth, seeking communion
with all who are free enough and pure enough
to behold them.

In our day the accursed hunger after gold,
and the no less accursed repletion of it, which
brings with it a stagnation of life, and ends in
an ossification of the whole heart, have rendered
us less fit for the reception and proper cherishing
of the wondrous gifts of song.   But that the day
of poetry has gone by is no more true than that
the day of the soul has gone by, for they were
born, and must live and die, together.   The
soul mounts higher and higher, and its horizon
widens from age to age.   Poesy also grows
wiser as she grows older.   Poetry can never be
all written.   There is more in the heart of man
than any the wisest poet has ever seen there,—
more in the soul than any has ever guessed.
Our age may have no great poets, for there are
some who have but just now gone forth into
the silence, some who yet linger on the doubtful
brink, and there are successions in poesy as in
nature; pines spring up where oaks are cut

down,—the lyrical follows the epic. But of whatever kind or degree, there will ever yet be *some* poets. They are needed as historians of wonderful facts which, but for them, would be unrecorded,—facts high above the grasp of the diligent recorders of outward events; and materials of history will never be wanting to them since there is nothing so beautiful but has in it the promise of a higher beauty, nothing so true but enfolds the elements of a wider and more universal truth.

Trieste Publishing has a massive catalogue of classic book titles. Our aim is to provide readers with the highest quality reproductions of fiction and non-fiction literature that has stood the test of time. The many thousands of books in our collection have been sourced from libraries and private collections around the world.

The titles that Trieste Publishing has chosen to be part of the collection have been scanned to simulate the original. Our readers see the books the same way that their first readers did decades or a hundred or more years ago. Books from that period are often spoiled by imperfections that did not exist in the original. Imperfections could be in the form of blurred text, photographs, or missing pages. It is highly unlikely that this would occur with one of our books. Our extensive quality control ensures that the readers of Trieste Publishing's books will be delighted with their purchase. Our staff has thoroughly reviewed every page of all the books in the collection, repairing, or if necessary, rejecting titles that are not of the highest quality. This process ensures that the reader of one of Trieste Publishing's titles receives a volume that faithfully reproduces the original, and to the maximum degree possible, gives them the experience of owning the original work.

We pride ourselves on not only creating a pathway to an extensive reservoir of books of the finest quality, but also providing value to every one of our readers. Generally, Trieste books are purchased singly - on demand, however they may also be purchased in bulk. Readers interested in bulk purchases are invited to contact us directly to enquire about our tailored bulk rates. Email: customerservice@triestepublishing.com

You May Also Like

The Credibility of the Christian Religion; Or, Thoughts on Modern Rationalism

Samuel Smith

ISBN: 9780649557516
Paperback: 204 pages
Dimensions: 5.83 x 0.43 x 8.27 inches
Language: eng

Report of the Second Annual Meeting of the Maryland State Bar Association, Held at Ocean City, Maryland, July 28-29, 1897

Conway W. Sams

ISBN: 9780649724185
Paperback: 130 pages
Dimensions: 6.14 x 0.28 x 9.21 inches
Language: eng

www.triestepublishing.com

You May Also Like

Persecution and Tolerance: Being the Hulsean Lectures Preached Before the University of Cambridge in 1893-4

Mandell Creighton

ISBN: 9780649669356
Paperback: 164 pages
Dimensions: 6.14 x 0.35 x 9.21 inches
Language: eng

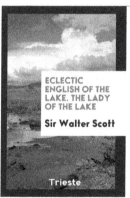

Eclectic English of the Lake. The Lady of the Lake

Sir Walter Scott

ISBN: 9780649623914
Paperback: 200 pages
Dimensions: 5.5 x 0.42 x 8.25 inches
Language: eng

www.triestepublishing.com

You May Also Like

ISBN: 9780649333158
Paperback: 84 pages
Dimensions: 6.14 x 0.17 x 9.21 inches
Language: eng

Report of the Department of Farms and Markets, pp. 5-71

Various

ISBN: 9780649324132
Paperback: 78 pages
Dimensions: 6.14 x 0.16 x 9.21 inches
Language: eng

Catalogue of the Episcopal Theological School in Cambridge Massachusetts, 1891-1892

Various

www.triestepublishing.com

You May Also Like

ISBN: 9780649352142
Paperback: 88 pages
Dimensions: 6.14 x 0.18 x 9.21 inches
Language: eng

Three Hundred Tested Recipes

Various

ISBN: 9780649419418
Paperback: 108 pages
Dimensions: 6.14 x 0.22 x 9.21 inches
Language: eng

A Basket of Fragments

Anonymous

Find more of our titles on our website. We have a selection of thousands of titles that will interest you. Please visit

www.triestepublishing.com

Lightning Source UK Ltd.
Milton Keynes UK
UKOW06f2055251017
311651UK00006B/723/P